MYASKOVSKY:
HIS LIFE AND WORK

Nikolai Yakovlevich Myaskovsky

MYASKOVSKY:
HIS LIFE AND WORK

by
ALEXEI A. IKONNIKOV

TRANSLATED FROM THE RUSSIAN

GREENWOOD PRESS, PUBLISHERS
NEW YORK

1 2 2 9 0 5

Foreword

The present work is designed to give no more than a general account of Myaskovsky's life and work, with particular reference to the genres cultivated by him, the peculiar features of his style and his place in the history of music. Some of his more outstanding individual compositions—particularly symphonies—are treated separately, but in the briefest possible manner.

The book was completed in the early part of 1941, when it was scheduled for publication. On account of the war, however, it was not printed.

In September, 1943, the author returned to the work and included an analysis of the music written by Myaskovsky since the beginning of the war. The result was a brief paper which has been appended to the present book in the form of a supplement. Pressure of work has unfortunately prevented the author from extending this supplement to include Myaskovsky's latest works—the Ninth String Quartet in E minor, Op. 62, and the 24th Symphony in F minor, Op. 63.

The author's sincerest acknowledgments are due to the composer, Nicholas Myaskovsky; Prof. B. V. Asafyev, Prof. A. A. Alschwang, Prof. D. B. Kabalevsky, and to the author's wife, V. M. Ikonnikova.

A. I.

May, 1944.

Contents

Biography

Nikolai Yakovlevich Myaskovsky was born on April 8 (April 20—New Style), 1881, in the fortress town of Novo-Georgiyevsk, Warsaw Gubernia.

His parents, Yakov Konstantinovich and Vera Nikolayevna, were linked by family tradition to military circles. The composer's grandfather, Konstantin Ivanovich Myaskovsky, had been a tutor at the Cadet College in Orel; his father had studied as a military engineer and later became a prominent specialist in fortification work, while Nikolai Petrakov, his maternal grandfather, had been a supervisor at a military gymnasium in Nizhni-Novgorod.

The Novo-Georgiyevsk Fortress, where Myaskovsky spent his early childhood, was in reality a small town surrounded by forts. Other forts were under construction, and the engineers in charge of the work lived in small, cosy cottages close to the building sites. It was in one of these cottages, standing in its own garden, that Yakov Konstantinovich, his wife and four children—two daughters,[1] Vera (1885) and Valentine (1886), and two sons, Sergei (1877) and Nikolai (1881)—had their home.

Yakov Konstantinovich, the composer's father, was noted for his modesty and assiduity. "These qualities of his," Myaskovsky recalls, "served as an example to his children. We not only respected our father but loved him dearly. The rare hours he spent with us were always precious, and we have never forgotten them."

---

[1] A third daughter, Eugenia, was born in Kazan in 1890.

Vera Nikolayevna, the mother, died while still young—in 1890—and left a deep impression of kindness and tenderness on Myaskovsky's memory. After her death, the children were taken care of by their father's sister, Yelikonida Konstantin-ovna Myaskovskaya. An atmosphere of mutual affection continued to reign in the Myaskovsky home, where there was a long-standing tradition of gentleness and tolerance in the relations between elders and children.

The children lived a free and spacious life, playing out-of-doors to their hearts' content. Their favorite game was pirates, and the eldest of them, Sergei, used to relegate the part of Pirate Chief to himself, leaving the others, including Nikolai, to "run errands" for him. This was not to Nikolai's liking, however, and he would often slink off by himself behind the walls of the forts and gather saltpeter for fireworks. Although he did not shun them altogether, Nikolai did not care for boisterous games. He preferred to play quietly indoors.

Above all, he loved to play with puppets. He would cut all sorts of figures out of cardboard, write his own plays, learn the rôles, compose the music and hum it through the teeth of a comb. Whenever anybody played the piano, there was no greater pleasure for Myaskovsky than to sit down "right underneath the piano," as he puts it, and listen.

No special importance was attached to music in the Myas-kovsky home, but, nevertheless, it had its place there. The children's mother had played the piano a little, their father sang operatic arias to them, while Yelikonida Konstantinovna had had a musical education. She had conducted the choir at the Yekaterininsky Institute and at one time had even sung in the chorus of the former Mariinsky Theatre. The children loved to hear her talk of life in St. Petersburg, and were overjoyed when she played the piano to them, or sang songs, in which they would often join. Yelikonida Konstantinovna was the future composer's first music teacher, and, as he himself admits, it was she who fired him with a love for his art.

One thing, however, clouded his happiness at this time. The strict religious atmosphere in the Myaskovsky home ruled out all games, music or recreation of any description on Saturdays and Sundays during the hours of divine service. In Nikolai's own words: "One of my gloomiest memories is of those long hours on Saturdays when our aunt used to lecture us. She would call us together and scold us unmercifully for all our misdeeds, for playing practical jokes, spoiling our clothes and disturbing our father (in her opinion we used to interrupt his work with our games). After these lectures, Auntie would mutter several times in succession, 'the Devil, the Devil, the Devil,' as if to exorcise the Evil One, the Tempter and Corrupter of Morals. She would then leave for vespers, from which she returned soothed and quieted." [2]

His aunt's religious mania, which was heightened by her nervous disorder—she was a prey to agoraphobia and dreaded open spaces—profoundly irritated Myaskovsky and led to an unhealthy reticence in him. He would lapse into moody silence for days and even weeks on end. At such times his father would come to the rescue and arrange a "reconciliation" between the boy and his aunt.

The family's stay in Orenburg (1888–1889) and in Kazan (1889–1893) marked Myaskovsky's first steps in education. During these years he began to take an interest in books and music; it was then that, having entered the Cadet Corps, he first embarked on a life of independence.

---

[2] From a conversation with Myaskovsky.—A. I.

Myaskovsky himself writes of this period as follows: [3]

"By now music was already a driving force. The decisive moment arrived when I heard a pianoforte duet (I can't remember by whom) of some piece that stirred me profoundly. I later found out, not without considerable pains, that it was a *potpourri* from Mozart's *Don Giovanni*.

"Then began my pleadings for a musical education. We finally hired a piano and Auntie began to teach me: but her nerves were bad and she was not consistent enough in her methods. As a result she tended to rely too much on my own receptiveness."

It is quite possible that the boy's eager desire to study music was accentuated by his impressions of various operas and operettas which he saw at the time. He remembers having been "profoundly impressed" by Verstovsky's *The Tomb of Ascold*, "overwhelmed" by Glinka's *Ivan Susanin*, but "left rather uncertain" by Borodin's *Prince Igor*. The repertory of the Summer Theatre, which was frequently visited by the whole Myaskovsky family, included the operettas *Orphée aux enfers*, *Die Fledermaus*, *Les Cloches de Corneville*, *Mademoiselle Nitouche* and *Green Island*.

During his music lessons (the first were in 1891, after the death of his mother), Myaskovsky revealed a good memory and ear for music. He actually enjoyed running lightly and nimbly through scales, exercises, and the Bertini *études*, and quickly memorized the music. When, at a later date, he had to learn similar pieces and *études* by the score, he found he had to take more pains with them.

His intellectual bent was early evidenced by his lively interest in books. Myaskovsky's father had inculcated a love

<hr>

[3] "Autobiographical Notes on My Creative Development," *Sovietskaya Muzyka* [Soviet Music], No. 6, 1936.

of reading in all his children, and often of an evening, when the whole family was gathered round the parlor table, he would fetch down one of his favorite books from the shelf and read to them aloud. Nikolai also liked to read alone, and for this purpose he would hide himself away in his father's large library, which was always open to him. At the age of nine, Nikolai entered the preparatory class of a school in Kazan. He never bothered to do his home-work, contenting himself with memorizing his lessons in class. After two years at this school (until the autumn of 1893), Myaskovsky left for Nizhni-Novgorod, where he entered the local Cadet College. Here he scored top marks in the entrance examinations and was accepted directly into the second class.

"My memories of those school years are . . . rather bitter. I found it tremendously easy to study and was never below second in class. But the musical instinct that was developing in me found only an occasional outlet. I had rather a good music teacher at the Nizhni-Novgorod Cadet College (Madame Latour), who foresaw plenty of success for me. But it wasn't easy to get the piano to myself. I was constantly chased away by senior students and my stubbornness often landed me in hot water." [4]

Myaskovsky conscientiously went through all the exercises, *études* and scales that his teacher required; but for himself, "for the good of his soul" as he puts it, he played all sorts of song "hits" from the popular operas of the day, "smuggling" the music from one of his aunts.

Both Nikolai and his brother Sergei, who was likewise a student at the Cadet College, spent the week ends with these aunts of theirs—sisters of their mother—who lived in a small

---

[4] *Ibid.*

house on Malaya Pokrovskaya Street. The two boys made
themselves quite at home there and thoroughly enjoyed every
moment of their visits.

According to the composer himself, his private interests
during the time he spent at the Nizhni-Novgorod Cadet
College (1893–1894) included reading, stamp collecting
and, above all, of course—his dominating passion—music.
Two years later, Nikolai continued his studies with the
Second Cadet College in St. Petersburg.

"If there was any change in my position (that is, with
regard to music) on my arrival in St. Petersburg," writes
Myaskovsky, "it was certainly not for the better. A teacher
by the name of Stuneyev—a relative of Glinka's wife—was
invited to teach me. But since he gave me my lessons at
home, I was unable to use any of the pianos at school, which
were assigned by the hour to those students who had their
music lessons there. They were often free, however, but
whenever I tried to take advantage of this fact, I was in-
evitably chased away by the masters. I used to resent this
passionately." [5]

The apartment into which the Myaskovskys moved was in
in a house on Aptekarsky Ostrov [Dispensers' Island], in the
neighborhood of the Botanical Gardens. Not far from the
house was the *Mon Plaisir* Summer Theatre, where symphony concerts were performed during the afternoons.
Myaskovsky enjoyed the concerts to such an extent that he
never missed a single program. One of the results of this new
infatuation was that he began to take violin lessons from a
member of the orchestra and was soon able to join the Cadet

[5] *Ibid.*

College amateur symphony orchestra as second violin. His piano lessons were temporarily forsaken.

A year later the family moved to another flat, this time in a house belonging to the State Engineering Department, which stood on the corner of Znamenskaya and Kirochnaya Streets. The flat was large and spacious, and the boys were able to spend their free hours at home, romping and playing music to their hearts' content.

But these free hours were few and far between, and Myaskovsky could devote little time to music except during the week ends, when he was free from school. At school he was handicapped by the fact that he was not officially studying with the music teacher there. Consequently he had to rest content with his activities in the College orchestra and an occasional opportunity to accompany a violinist friend of his. At home he also played for his cousin, Karl Bogdanovich Brandt, another violinist.

They played Mozart's E minor, B-flat minor and G major sonatas for piano and violin, Beethoven's F major and A major sonatas, and a whole series of miscellaneous serenades. Karl Bogdanovich was a member of an amateur German orchestra and often took Nikolai along to their concerts. "My cousin used to drag me there every Saturday and make me sit through whole evenings of symphonies by Kalliwoda, Onslow and the like. Once, however, I was amazed when I heard the overture to Rossini's *William Tell*, with the famous flute solo at the beginning. And I was absolutely knocked off my feet by Beethoven's Second Symphony, especially the *larghetto*." [6]

---

[6] *Ibid.*

The Myaskovsky flat on Znamenskaya Street was often visited by the Gorodenskys—friends and relatives of the family from Helsingfors.[7] Myaskovsky would spend hour after hour playing pianoforte duets with the mother and daughter, usually taking the second part. They played symphonies, overtures by Mendelssohn, Haydn, Beethoven, Schubert, Schumann, and a host of other transcriptions.

During this period Myaskovsky began to take his first lessons in harmony from N. Kazanli, the conductor of the College orchestra.

Prompted by his frequent visits to concerts and his constant association with musicians, Myaskovsky—at the age of fifteen—decided to try his own hand at composition. His first creative efforts resulted in a few preludes for the piano, which later swelled into a whole album. They were played only to Maria Vasilyevna Gorodenskaya—his sole confidante in matters of music. The composer himself only recalls in detail one of these preludes now—after a nocture by Chopin (Op. 15, No. 3)—but, from their general character, it seems clear that these early compositions were evidence of his serious attitude to music at the time.

Another landmark in the development of this young enthusiast, who did not even dream as yet of becoming a professional musician or composer, was a Tchaikovsky concert conducted by Arthur Nikisch (December, 1896). The program, which included the Sixth Symphony and the symphonic poem, *Voyevoda*, left a profound impression on Myaskovsky.

---

[7] Alexandra Ivanovna Gorodenskaya was an accomplished composer. Her daughter, Maria Vasilyevna Gorodenskaya, was Myaskovsky's permanent partner in pianoforte duets for four hands.

The score of Tchaikovsky's symphony, which was given to him as a present, became the future composer's inseparable companion. From then on Myaskovsky did not miss a single symphony concert arranged by the Russian Musical Society, but attended them regularly right up to the time of his graduation from the Cadet College.

"My graduation from the Cadet College in 1899 marked me out for a military career, for which I had nothing but the strongest distaste, and to which I had been doomed by family and social tradition alone. I accordingly entered the school which was the least military in spirit—the School of Military Engineering, which at the time was under the liberal (from the military point of view) supervision of the historian General N. K. Schilder. Of all the military training schools I attended it is the only one that I can recall now with the minimum of disgust. The reason for this lies in the fact that it was here that I received my *greatest musical stimulus* [italics mine—A. I.], and that I had more time at my disposal. The school accepted only the best students from the College and, as a result, in addition to a large percentage of 'crammers' and careerists, it also catered to a number of really intelligent young people.

"I had the good fortune to come across a whole group of music enthusiasts, followers of a trend in music—the 'Big Five' [8]—which was totally unfamiliar to me.

"V. L. Modzalevsky, brother of the well-known Pushkin scholar; V. L. Hofmann, brother of another authority on Pushkin, and N. N. Sukharzhevsky, an exceedingly talented 'cellist (a pupil of Wierzbolowwicz) and a composer of sorts,

---

[8] Moussorgsky, Borodin, Rimsky-Korsakov, Cui and Balakirev.

constituted the kernel of our group, which also included
members of their families. Some of the latter were professional musicians." [9]

The friends gathered once or twice a week at the homes
of Modzalevsky and Hofmann. Precisely from this period
music became a dominating influence in Myaskovsky's life
and then it was that the future composer became well acquainted for the first time with the Russian classics—of
Borodin, Rimsky-Korsakov, Balakirev, Moussorgsky and
Glazounov (Glinka was already known to him). Moreover,
there was no branch of music in which the friends were not
interested: opera, symphonies, quartets and romances.

Myaskovsky's acquaintance with the works of the composers comprising the "Big Five" was of primary importance
not so much because it enabled him to extend his knowledge
of music, but because it diverted his interest from the German masters to Russian music. Glinka, Moussorgsky,
Rimsky-Korsakov and Tchaikovsky became his most cherished inspiration.

On leaving the School of Military Engineering in 1902,
Myaskovsky was enrolled in the Second Reserve Sappers
Battalion in the town of Zaraisk, and a month later in the
17th Sappers Battalion in Moscow. From the autumn of 1902
to January, 1903, he acquainted himself with Moscow, attended concerts and did a little composing (the F minor
Fantasia for piano). Having broken out of the "hateful walls"
of the school into the comparative freedom of the great city,
Myaskovsky began to look for ways and means of resuming
his musical studies, "now, however, only in the field of composition, for I felt that the experiments I had made so far in

---

9 "Autobiographical Notes."

this field lagged far behind my general musical development and left much to be desired." [10]

With this object Myaskovsky obtained a recommendation from Rimsky-Korsakov to Taneyev who, in turn, referred him to his pupil R. M. Glière, a recent graduate from the Moscow Conservatory.

Myaskovsky studied harmony with Glière from January to May, 1903. Meanwhile, he composed a number of romances to verses selected at random "for himself." One of these has been preserved, a *Lullaby* composed to words by Balmont. The summer of 1903 was taken up with field maneuvers, and in the autumn Myaskovsky was transferred back to St. Petersburg, to the 18th Sappers Battalion, where he again found himself "under his father's wing." Acting on Glière's advice, he continued his studies in St. Petersburg, under I. I. Kryzhanovsky, a graduate of Rimsky-Korsakov's composition class.

One of the most vivid impressions he carried away with him from Moscow was of Rimsky-Korsakov's opera, *Kashchei, the Immortal,* a new production at the time. It was the "unusual" in the opera that fascinated Myaskovsky, the whole world of fantasy which it revealed, expressed with the aid of new and uncommon musical devices.

As a composer, Myaskovsky now acquired a new characteristic trait in the form of a strong inclination for progressive trends. This tendency was strengthened by his association and studies with Kryzhanovsky. The latter, who was himself attracted to all that was progressive in music not only with regard to methods of expression but also with regard to content—a musician with "an inborn flair for the new"—could

[10] *Ibid.*

not but command Myaskovsky's respect. Kryzhanovsky's influence on the future composer was considerable, but of a
rather broad and general character. Without plunging into
technical details, however, he gave Myaskovsky, who studied
with him from the autumn of 1903 to the spring of 1906, an
excellent general grasp of his art. The subjects he touched on
included not only composition, counterpoint, fugues and
musical forms, but also orchestration.

On his arrival in St. Petersburg Myaskovsky returned to
his circle of "temporairly forsaken friends." The Hofmann
flat continued to be a miniature center of literature and music
for them, and they gathered here, as before, to play music,
read poetry and discuss the latest news in the world of art.

The literary provender of the circle was supplied by read-
ings from the journals *Vesy* [Scales], *Mir Iskusetva* [World
of Art], and *Zolotoye Runo* [Golden Fleece], interspersed
with volumes from the Pirozhkov series of contemporary
writers. At the same time Myaskovsky read Maxim Gorky,
Skitalets, Leonid Andreyev and other more democratic
writers. Every new book and composition was hotly debated.
During this period Myaskovsky became acquainted with
Vyacheslav Ivanov, Sergei Gorodetsky, Mikhail Kuzmin and
other poets.

Modernist literature now threw its spell over Myaskovsky
(1903–1906). He read Balmont, Zinaida Gippius, Merezh-
kovsky, Sologub and others, and composed many songs to
works by the Russian symbolists. That year, besides a number of romances, he wrote two fantasias for the piano, a pianoforte sonata and the first part of a quartet (unfinished), in
addition to orchestrating Tchaikovsky's pianoforte pieces,
Op. 21.

Kryzhanovsky was amazed by the remarkable psychological

intuition and subtlety of expression that characterized Myaskovsky's romances to words by Zinaida Gippius, and used them to introduce the latter to the "Evenings of Modern Music" society. The main sponsors of these evenings were V. G. Karatygin, A. D. Medem, A. P. Nurok and W. F. Nuvel.

Pokrovsky the pianist, Senilov the composer, Yovanovich, a pianist and singer, and Yanovsky were among those who participated in the activities of the society.

The older generation of composers (Rimsky-Korsakov, Lyadov and Glazounov) were represented at the "Evenings" only on those occasions when their works were featured on the program, and were inclined to be skeptical of the whole business. Myaskovsky kept in the background, preferring just to listen.

The high demands made by the members of the society on the composers of their day, combined with his insufficient knowledge of the technical processes of composition, aroused in Myaskovsky a strong feeling of dissatisfaction with his musical training. These attacks of what he termed "nightmares of literacy" subsequently led to the destruction of a large quantity of his works, which he himself branded as "immature." At the same time it was being brought home to him more and more forcibly that he had to make up his mind once and for all with regard to the profession he should follow. There seemed to be only one path toward the accomplishment of his goal: the Conservatory.

"My first serious attempts at composing," Myaskovsky recalls,[11] "put me in touch with the foremost musicians grouped around the 'Evenings of Modern Music.' True, I did

---

[11] *Ibid.*

not become one of them, so to speak, since then, as now, the tireless quest for the *dernier cri* in musical technique and invention did not constitute an end in itself for me.

"At any rate, the atmosphere of tense musical searching there and the stern evaluation of each finished composition could not but affect me and make me feel that I was still a dilettante and that, so long as I remained bound to the military service that weighed so heavily upon me, I should never be able to find a way out of my predicament.

"From this period my conscious struggle for my own independent musical existence became still more stubborn."

Myaskovsky's yearning to devote himself to music became imperative. While still confined within the walls of the School of Military Engineering, he had already come to look with abhorrence on the idea of adopting the army as a career; now that he had become independent and had strengthened his ties with the musical world, he found his military connections infinitely more irksome. Accordingly, in the spring of 1905, he handed in a formal application for permission to enter the Academy of Law, ostensibly in order to continue his studies.[12] By this means he was able to avoid attending camp that year under the pretext of preparing for his "entrance exams." Actually, however, he plunged "furiously" into the task of writing some new romances and morceaux for the pianoforte. During the two or three months of the summer he composed *The Knock, Inscription in a Book, Lands of Despondency, The Christian, The Moon and the Mist*, and *Contradiction*, all to words of Zinaida Gippius, as well as a C minor pianoforte sonata in three

---

[12] Graduates from the School of Military Engineering were permitted to continue their studies either in military science in military academies, or in law in the Academy of Law.

movements (which he subsequently destroyed). In the autumn, when the entrance examinations were due to begin, Myaskovsky was obliged to "fall ill."

Although at home the family subscribed to the conservative papers, Myaskovsky took out the *Novaya Zhizn* [New Life]. He also read avidly the political and philosophical articles that appeared regularly in such magazines as the *Polyarnaya Zvezda* [Polar Star]. It must be pointed out that this predilection of his for what was progressive in literature, social events and music sprang in the main from his own personal qualities. Neither his environment at home nor the military circles to which he was attached by sheer necessity helped him in this respect. If he received any external impetus, this could only have come from his participation in the Hofmann gatherings.

"The summer of 1906 was spent in preparing for the Conservatory which I had firmly decided to enter—even as an external student if need be, since I was still bound by my military service." [13]

The winter of 1906 and spring of 1907 marked the end of Myaskovsky's term of military service and the beginning of his studies at the St. Petersburg Conservatory.

At his entrance examinations Myaskovsky, who was twenty-five at the time, was confronted with a formidable array of musical celebrities: Rimsky-Korsakov, Glazounov and Lyadov were among the chief examiners. "Rimsky-Korsakov tested my ear for music—I had to define certain notes and chords and repeat one or two melodies by ear. This went off without a hitch. Then I had to play my C minor sonata (in three movements). . . . This also passed smoothly enough. Things

---

[13] "Autobiographical Notes."

began to take a less favorable turn when it came to the question of my musical tastes." It appeared that, as a disciple of Kryzhanovsky, Myaskovsky was a partisan of contemporary music and "recognized" such composers as Reger, Richard Straus and, "doubtless," as Rimsky-Korsakov ironically remarked, "even enjoyed the famous passage from *Salome*" (at one point in the opera the major scales of B-flat and D are rendered simultaneously). Rimsky-Korsakov sat down there and then at the piano and demonstrated the offending passage, and Myaskovsky was obliged to "give Strauss up" out of tactical considerations, in order not to offend the examiners by a display of his own tastes. The most dangerous test was to come, however, when he tackled the harmonization of a chorale, over which he very nearly came to grief. The situation was saved only by his well-written modulation prelude to a theme given him by Glazounov.

His work at the Conservatory was arranged as follows: counterpoint and harmony with Lyadov, orchestration with Rimsky-Korsakov, and piano, which was obligatory, with Winkler. At the same time Myaskovsky managed to cope with his military duties that occupied most of his daylight hours. . . . "I had to display phenomenal resourcefulness in order to be at the job on time, miss no lessons and, in addition, put in a great deal of work. . . ." [14]

Myaskovsky's stamina and efficiency produced brilliant results. He not only studied well: he managed to do much more than was required of him. He even found time to go to concerts.

His first year at the Conservatory brought Myaskovsky many new friends, among whom were B. V. Asafyev, S. S.

---

[14] *Ibid.*

Prokofieff, L. I. Saminsky, now a well-known composer and conductor in the United States; Y. S. Akimenko (who subsequently made a name for himself as the Ukrainian composer, Y. Stepovy), Lvov, Rozovsky, and others.

In the spring of 1907 Myaskovsky's term of compulsory military service came to an end. He handed in his resignation, much to the chagrin of his father, who had set his heart on his son's becoming a military engineer.

The summer vacation following this year of hard work was devoted to creative activity. He wrote the first and second movements of his D minor pianoforte sonata, the B major sonata in five parts, twelve morceaux for the piano,[15] seven romances to words by Baratynsky, which later constituted his Opus 1, and an F major string quartet in four movements.

During the same summer he coached one of his school friends—A. N. Kobylyansky—in harmony for the entrance examinations to the St. Petersburg Conservatory. Kobylyansky is now a professor of the pianoforte at the Leningrad Conservatory. This was Myaskovsky's first step in his pedagogical career.

The composer had "rested" no less industriously during his vacations in the previous winter and spring (1906–1907). The winter was devoted to the composition of two one-movement pianoforte sonatas (G major and C minor) and twelve piano pieces.[16]

In the autumn of 1907 Myaskovsky lost nearly two months of study by reason of an attack of appendicitis and an operation. On his recovery he attended Lyadov's class in fugues (1907–1908) and continued to study orchestration under Rimsky-Korsakov and the pianoforte with Winkler. During

---

[15] "Frolics," Book III.   [16] "Frolics," Books I and II.

the winter and spring vacations of that year he composed the piano pieces entitled *Frolics,* later .revised and printed as *Reminiscences* (Op. 29); *Yellowed Leaves* (Op. 31) and several pieces from Opus 43. He also wrote the first movement of his A-flat major sonata and several songs to Zinaida Gippius' *Circles, Blood* and other verses. The same winter also saw the beginning of his work on his First Symphony, which was completed in the summer of 1908.

At the beginning of the next academic year (Myaskovsky's third year of studies) he showed the score of his symphony to Glazounov, who praised its "maturity of thought" and, in token of his approval, granted its author, who was in difficulty with his fees at the time, a minor scholarship.

On completing his course in harmony, counterpoint and fugues in his third year at the Conservatory, Myaskovsky took up the structure of musical forms under Jazeps Vitols, now one of Latvia's leading composers. For purposes of practice, Myaskovsky discussed with Vitols some of his own piano and vocal compositions, including one or two that he wrote especially for the class. These included the romances to Vyacheslav Ivanov's *Pan and Psyche, Temple-Valley, The Storm* and parts of the D minor pianoforte sonata, Opus 6.

From the summer of 1909 up to the spring of 1911—his year of graduation from the Conservatory—Myaskovsky was engaged on the symphonic poem, *The Vow of Silence* (after Edgar Allan Poe), scored for an enlarged symphony orchestra; the *Petite Ouverture* in G major (for orchestra), based on the G major pianoforte sonata, which was criticized in its time by Kryzhanovsky for its artificial *style russe;* the *Sinfonietta* in A major (Op. 10) scored for a small symphony orchestra and consisting of three movements: (a) *Waltz,* (b) *Idyll,* and (c) *Rondo,* written under the influence of

Mozart's *Eine Kleine Nachtmusik*; the first movement of the Second Symphony (in C-sharp minor, Op. 11); the F minor string quartet in four movements (Op. 33, No. 4); the D minor string quartet in two movements (Op. 33, No. 3); the music to a sonnet by Michelangelo (Tyutchev's translation); and *Madrigal*—five romances to words by Balmont.

In the spring of 1911 Myaskovsky graduated from the Conservatory. He had now won the right to the calling of composer. The hardest part of the way (his break with the army and his home traditions) lay behind him. During the years spent in the Conservatory, Myaskovsky had made yet another vital decision, inseparably bound up with the first: he had chosen his path as a composer, and it was the symphonic path. During the very first summer following his graduation he composed his Second Symphony, which laid the foundations for his *independent creative activity,* for his work was now both mature and original. Through the medium of K. Sarajev, the conductor, and V. Derzhanovsky, the critic, Myaskovsky was introduced to the Moscow public both as a composer (Sarajev was the first to conduct his symphonic poem, *The Vow of Silence,* at Sokolniki, in 1911) and as a music critic (Derzhanovsky invited him to contribute to the music column in the new weekly *Muzyka* [Music]). Myaskovsky contributed to this magazine until 1914.

In the summer of 1911 Myaskovsky composed his only sonata for 'cello and piano (Op. 12); in 1912, a symphonic poem in C minor; *Alastor,* after Shelley (Op. 14), and his Second Pianoforte sonata in F-sharp minor (actually his seventh); in 1913 he wrote his Third Symphony in A minor (Op. 15), and romances to Zinaida Gippius' *Gift, Pain, Is It So?, Incantation, Unawares* and *The Cocks*; finally, in 1914, he worked on the orchestration of his Third Symphony.

The outbreak of the First World War marked a radical change in the composer's life, and he found himself in the front-line positions in Galicia, near Lvov and Przemysl.

"My participation in the war and certain new acquaintances I made there, served in great measure to strengthen my democratic views, which had taken shape while I was still at the Conservatory, and which had become positive enough, though not yet quite crystallized, in the days of the February Revolution. The July events in Leningrad, however, which reached Revel through the press, caused me to swing instinctively to a definite radical position." [17]

In these simple words Myaskovsky refers to the events of 1917 and touches lightly on his own reactions to them. But his activities, from the very first day of the existence of the Soviet state, testify, more than any words, to the full force and purport that the Revolution had for him.

Myaskovsky remained in the naval fortress of Revel (Tallinn) from February, 1917 to the end of the year when, as the result of an illness (he had been shell shocked), he was transferred to the Naval Staff at St. Petersburg. Upon his arrival there in December, he began to work on his Fourth Symphony, which he finished as soon as February, 1918. His Fifth Symphony rapidly followed the Fourth, but was not orchestrated until his transfer (together with the Naval Staff), from St. Petersburg to Moscow. This took place in the winter of 1919.

The war broadened the composer's outlook, bringing him closer to reality. New trends appeared in his work, evidenced by a quieter and simpler musical language, akin to folk music.

---

[17] *Ibid.*

At the end of 1919 he became a member of the Bureau of Composers—the first organization of musicians in Soviet Russia.

In 1921 Myaskovsky simultaneously filled the positions of Assistant Director of the Music Department of the People's Commissariat of Education and professor at the Moscow State Conservatory. After being released from his work at the People's Commissariat of Education in 1922, he was appointed editor and juryman of the Music Publishing House, where he worked until 1931. At the same time he became a member of the Art Section of the State Education Council, and subsequently a member of the Academy of Arts.

Contributing all his knowledge and energy to his manifold administrative and organizational activities, Myaskovsky, like the genuine Soviet citizen and worker that he was, actively participated in the building up of Soviet musical culture. And the path he traversed as an artist was even more arduous and no less purposeful.

After writing his outstanding Sixth Symphony (1922–1923) which in its own way reflected the majestic and formidable march of the Revolution with all its victories and sacrifices, Myaskovsky composed a series of works testifying to the intricate processes of development taking place in his artistic and social outlook.

The 12th or "Collective-Farm" Symphony (1931), which he dedicated to the Fifteenth Anniversary of the October Revolution, constitutes an important landmark in his career. This work, based on the Soviet theme of collectivization, proved to be an event of the greatest importance both for the composer himself and for Soviet music as a whole. The 12th Symphony posed the question of bringing Soviet music and the symphonic genre in particular onto the broad path of realist art.

If in the 12th Symphony this problem is not completely solved, the subsequent works of the composer, beginning with the 14th and 15th Symphonies, testify to the great successes achieved by him in the sphere of Socialist realism in art.

From 1935 to 1940 Myaskovsky worked on his popular lyrical-heroic 16th Symphony, the dramatic 17th (which, we regret to say, is very rarely performed), the folk-song 18th, the 19th, 20th and 21st Symphonies, a violin concerto, two string quartets, and two cycles of romances to words by Lermontov and Shchipachev.

While engaged in this tremendous creative activity Myaskovsky, like his famous predecessors Rimsky-Korsakov, Lyadov and Glazounov, continued no less intensively to participate in the work of building up the musical culture and musical education in his country. He holds a leading position in the Union of Soviet Composers, is consultant for music broadcasts on the All-Union Radio Committee, and works on the editorial staff of the periodical, *Sovietskaya Muzyka*. His pedagogical labors extend far beyond the precincts of the Moscow State Conservatory. His home is never without visitors—musicians, pedagogues, students and composers—to whom he freely offers advice. Myaskovsky's weighty judgments and deep musical culture, combined with his exceptional modesty, have earned him the profound respect of all Soviet musicians.

Throughout the years of Soviet power he has permanently held the post of Professor of Composition at the Tchaikovsky State Conservatory in Moscow. He has brought up two generations of talented composers and musicians who have won recognition both in the Soviet Union and abroad. In this respect he may well be compared with his own teachers— N. A. Rimsky-Korsakov and A. K. Lyadov. During the twenty years of his professional activity Myaskovsky has graduated more than forty composers, including Alexandrov, Bely, Vitachek, Hamburg, Kabalevsky, Muradeli, Polovinkin, Khachaturyan, Shebalin and many others, some of whom have, in their turn, already graduated another generation of composers.

In connection with the 60th anniversary of the Moscow State Conservatory (1926), the title of Artist of Merit of the R.S.F.S.R. was conferred upon Myaskovsky and his colleagues Goldenweiser, Neuhaus and Igumnov. On January 3, 1940, the Higher Diploma Commission of the All-Union Committee on Higher Education conferred on Myaskovsky the honorary degree of Doctor of Arts.

In recognition of his 21st Symphony Myaskovsky was awarded the Stalin Prize of the First Degree by an edict of the Council of People's Commissars of the U.S.S.R., dated March 15, 1941.

Myaskovsky made the following short but profoundly significant statement in acknowledgment of the honor bestowed upon him:

"The award of the Stalin Prizes for music is a proud and happy occasion for us all. The list of winners this year consists largely of artists of the older and middle generations. And in the future, too, we, the 'old hands,' will not lightly relinquish this great honor, and will strive to retain our position at the head of the list. Nevertheless, I wish from the bottom of my heart that in this friendly competition between brother artists victory should remain in future with our boundlessly talented youth, which will be called upon to create the first music of Communist society and the best music in the world." [18]

Myaskovsky, as a representative of the older generation, has every right to challenge the forces of youth in the great task of building up a genuine Socialist art. He has every right—for he himself occupies a place of honor among the builders of the musical culture of the first classless society in the world.

[18] *Sovietskoye Iskusetva* [Soviet Art], No. 12, 1941.

Creative Activity

SYMPHONIC WORKS

Symphony No. 1 in C minor, Opus 3

Myaskovsky's First Symphony was written during the summer of 1908, after he had been studying at the Conservatory for two years. This was his first essay in the larger orchestral forms and represented a certain stage in the composer's growth to maturity. It was not entirely original in style, but it showed beyond doubt that Myaskovsky already had a grasp of the symphonic form. The musical ideas in each movement are vividly expressed and so developed that the work as a whole has finish and unity.

The continuity of the three movements is ensured by the lucid tonal plan of C minor—A-flat major—C minor.

The first movement, with its spontaneous outbursts of feeling and romantic unrest, is followed by a tranquil, flowing *larghetto*, full of nobility and beauty. This is perhaps the most successful of the three movements. The finale is reminiscent of the first movement, but with more powerful rhythms and greater mobility.

It is the youthful freshness of this symphony that appeals to us, although the composer was nearly thirty when he wrote it. Its defects cannot be overlooked—the melodic line is sometimes blurred in the development of the thematic material, although the exposition of each theme separately is entirely clear and concise. This is evident chiefly in the thematic elaborations of the first and third movements, where the melodic line is often broken by unruly chord progressions and polyphonic devices, as a result of which these two movements have moments of artificiality.

Symphony No. 2 in C-sharp minor, Opus 11

Between 1909 and 1913 Myaskovsky produced six pieces for symphony orchestra—two more symphonies (Second Symphony in C-sharp minor, Third Symphony in A minor), two symphonic poems entitled *The Vow of Silence* (a fairy tale) and *Alastor*; a *Sinfonietta* (A major) and a *Petite Ouverture* (G major).

The Second Symphony in C-sharp minor is an important landmark in Myaskovsky's work. If the first movement is considerably influenced by Tchaikovsky and the second by Scriabin, the finale is Myaskovsky in the process of finding himself. Here is the chromatic opening theme, laconic and angular, so typical of the later Myaskovsky. Here, too, are many other features that we have come to associate with his work, impelling rhythms and "prickly" harmonies, coupled with a polyphonic development already masterly. With these, and above all, with that powerful expression of somber feeling peculiar to the composer, the finale of the Second Symphony is an assertion of those individual qualities which were but slightly perceptible in the First Symphony—a work that was far less characteristic in this respect than the tone poem, *The Vow of Silence.*

A review which appeared in the *Birzheviye Novosti* [Exchange News] on June 29, 1913, under the initials "A. K." may be of interest here: "He [Myaskovsky] has already come forward with a second symphony, a work of an extremely somber character. The only bright theme (*cantabile*) in the finale is all but drowned in a sea of dark, dissonant harmonies. I must also draw attention to the complexity and abruptness of this new work and its lack of contrast. . . . It contains many interesting pages, but these are only pages, and, taken as a whole, the symphony is merely a fine promise, not something complete in itself. It is a good sign, however, that the composer is in the grip of moods rather than a slave to empty musical forms. Here, we feel, is real suffering, emotion, blood from the heart. This is art that springs from life, not from some arid school."

Another review of Myaskovsky's work appeared in *Russkaya Molva* [Russian Talk], June 30, 1913, this time by I. I. Kryzhanovsky, who was his first teacher, and who continued to be his guide and friend for many years "The composer has a quite definite musical style, the characteristics of which on the one hand are dark moods sometimes re-echoing the anguished moments of Tchaikovsky and on the other hand ecstatic outbursts akin to those of Scriabin. . . .

"His interesting thematic material, his skill in the development and elaboration of themes, and his command of the orchestra, single out this young composer and lead us to expect much from his further efforts."

Kryzhanovsky, who knew Myaskovsky well from many other works, was naturally in a better position than others to estimate the prospects of Myaskovsky's future development.

After hearing his Second Symphony, the critics in both Moscow and St. Petersburg commented on Myaskovsky's originality.

"Among contemporary young composers," wrote S. Rozovsky, "with their craze for color and tasty musical tidbits, and general disregard for the real essence of music, Myaskovsky stands out with his pathos, refined spiritual experiences and lyric contemplativeness. . . ."

"Myaskovsky," noted the Moscow critic, George Konius, "apart from two or three passages in the finale (including the closing chord), has the courage not to follow the fashion and refuses to cater to the modern market which, as is known, has virtually no appreciation for anything but harmonic novelties and aberrations. . . ."

But in these early works Myaskovsky's gifts were not yet fully disclosed.

The Tone Poem Alastor, *Opus 14*

Of far greater significance are the Third Symphony and the symphonic poem, *Alastor*. "Virtually all these compositions," says Myaskovsky, "bear the imprint of a profound pessimism, as for example, my Second Pianoforte Sonata [F-sharp minor] written in 1912. I myself find it difficult to analyze the cause. Probably it was not far removed from the circumstances of my private life, as virtually to the age of thirty I had to struggle to disentangle myself from an environment which was all but hostile to the arts. At the same time there was an inner struggle to free myself from the thick cobwebs of dilettantism which enmeshed my first steps (and not only my first steps) in the career which I had chosen. On the other hand, there was a certain contact, though extremely superficial, with the symbolists, 'communal individualists,' and similar circles. Ideologically they did, of course, exert a certain influence on my somewhat raw psychology." [1]

One could hardly disagree with this statement. But it is far from complete. It says nothing of other features of Myaskovsky's music which offer considerable interest and are strikingly developed in his later works.

Even in the gloomiest of Myaskovsky's works the darkness is rent by fierce flashes of human passion and the visions of a questing mind in search of happiness. The tone poem *Alastor* tells the romantic story of a noble youth whom Shelley, and Myaskovsky a century later, endowed with some of the finest qualities of the human spirit: indomitable will, courage, pride and zest for knowledge. The ambition to know the world burns in Alastor like a torch. He studies the sciences and travels through many lands in his endeavor to unravel the laws of the universe. He is a solitary being, aloof from wordly vanities. Then Alastor sees in a dream the entrancing vision of a woman. She awakens love within his heart. Alastor, alone in the wilderness, tries to find her and dies with the fall of night.

In the single movement of this tone poem, Myaskovsky has succeeded in translating the philosophical content of the poem without digressions into descriptive music. We hear Alastor's proud strivings, his restless urge to seek and find, the lyrical tenderness of his dream, and, finally, his death— all these expressing an idea of lofty significance: the quest of art for knowledge of the world, the attraction of the artist toward the Byronic ideal for which even death is witness to the strength of the human spirit and intellect. Despite the

---

[1] "Autobiographical Notes."

gloomy tone of the work, Alastor's vitality and dynamic impetuosity form the dominant mood of the poem as a whole.

Symphony No. 3 in A minor, Opus 15

And such in essence is also the mood of the Third Symphony of Myaskovsky. Here is the composer's own analysis of the thematic material: "Introduction—a *motif* not without weight, of a rather menacing character, more often than not serving as the bass for the second theme in its main heroic form. A sinister theme (opening bars of subordinate subject) . . . hinted at here and there in the first movement but assuming a vast importance in the finale, where it becomes, as it were, the mainspring of the psychological collisions which are the nucleus of the movement and, indeed, of the whole symphony. . . .

"The main theme of the second movement is fiery and mobile . . . while the first subordinate theme (of the same movement) is of a languorous and passionate character. The conclusion is stern and subdued." [2]

The gloomy tone of the dénouement (funeral march) cannot be denied. But Myaskovsky does not bow impotently to fate. The grandeur of the opening theme of the symphony (scored for six French horns in unison), the irresistible power of the main theme of the first movement, the defiance and vigor of the first theme of the second movement—these plunge the listener into a maelstrom of emotions and revolt which grows and deepens until the fiery music fuses into a

---

[2] "N. Myaskovsky's Third Symphony in A Minor," a Thematic Analysis. *Sovremennaya Muzyka* [Contemporary Music], No. 27, 1928, pp. 97, 100, 101. This article, which is unsigned, was written by Myaskovsky himself.

single organic whole and flows on in a broad stream of musical inspiration.

Symphony No. 4 in E minor, Opus 17

After completing his Third Symphony, Myaskovsky planned another "in the barest outlines" as a "quiet" [3] piece "after the revolts and exaggerated emotions of my Second (1911) and Third (1913) Symphonies." [4] The idea of this symphony, which eventually materialized as his Fifth, was prevented from coming to fruition at the time, first, by the composer's departure to the front, and, second, by the Fourth Symphony, which was written between December, 1917, and February, 1918, immediately after his return home at the end of the war. "On returning to Petrograd at the end of 1917," writes Myaskovsky himself, "I resumed work not on the symphony I had been planning but on a more vigorous piece *as a reflection of what I had just been through* [italics mine—A. I.]—only with a happier ending. This was my Fourth Symphony." [5]

It is this symphony, perhaps, that expresses most fully the elements of musical style which were characteristic of this period of Myaskovsky. Regardless of the markedly functional nature of the music which makes entirely clear to both ear and mind the moments of tension and of climax; regardless, too, of the clear tonality of the work as a whole, the symphony abounds in dissonant harmonies. These discordant passages, as B. V. Asafyev has correctly pointed out, [6] should not be

[3] From a letter to the author, October 2, 1935.
[4] "Autobiographical Notes."
[5] *Ibid.*
[6] "Myaskovsky as a Symphonist." *Sovremennaya Muzyka*, No. 3, 1924.

attributed to any striving on the part of the composer after colorful effects, but must simply be regarded as incidental results of the voice-leading. At the same time the main lines of the voice-leading, in their turn, depend largely on the general chromatic structure of the themes.

The melody thus tends to become abrupt, and to lose its *cantabile* quality. As a result, except in the middle, slow movement of the symphony, it is built up not on any broadly developed melodic lines, but on one or two central phrases or groups. This, however, does not deprive it of its essentially rich and varied character.

Myaskovsky's use of harmonic sequences is no less significant in this respect. Coupled with the disjointedness of the melody, the use of sequences could not but increase the emotional tenseness of the music, and this is fully true of the first movement.

"The second movement," to quote the composer's own words, "is slow, very short, and of a stern and concentrated character, relieved by an occasional outburst of lyric emotion. The third and last movement is a spirited and energetic rondo." [7]

On the whole, the Fourth Symphony, tense, nervous and in a tone of almost unrelieved sternness, profoundly reflects the composer's state of mind at the time as an echo of the near past, *i.e.*, of his experiences during the war.

Symphony No. 5 in D major, Opus 18

In 1918 Myaskovsky wrote his Fifth Symphony. The following is the opinion of a foreign critic, Dr. Paul Pisk, quoted

---

[7] Thematic analysis of the Fourth and Seventh Symphonies. *Sovremennaya Muzyka*, No. 8, 1925, p. 38.

in the *Muzyka i Revolutzia* [Music and Revolution], No. 3, 1928, p. 45. It was written on the occasion of the first performance of the Fifth Symphony in Vienna. "It is hard to imagine a concert in which a new work performed for the first time has been so sympathetically received and with such enthusiastic approval. The audience felt that this symphony, well known in Russia and successful in America, has not, for all its complexity, lost contact with the folk spirit. In all four movements of his symphony Myaskovsky uses themes close to the folk idiom and gives expression to them in a truly Russian manner. The themes are so straightforward that they are readily comprehensible despite the consummate artistic skill and intricacy of their treatment."

Thus musical criticism in Western Europe noted the folk element and fundamental simplicity of musical idea as characteristic of the Fifth Symphony. It is, indeed, precisely in these features that the Fifth Symphony differs materially from Myaskovsky's earlier symphonic compositions.

Myaskovsky had no program in mind for the Fifth Symphony. "The whole symphony was a relaxation for me. In idea, it was a reaction to the Second and Third Symphonies, and in carrying out this idea I was having a rest from the Fourth Symphony." [8]

There are two significant themes in the first movement— the principal theme and the traditional subordinate theme of the normal sonata allegro. The first of these is a tranquil and smoothly flowing pastoral. The second is in the broad, somewhat austere style, characteristic of certain Russian folk melodies. The andante, in ternary form, is based on a melody akin to a Russian cradle song (except for the middle section,

---

[8] From a letter to the author, October 2, 1935.

which consists of a broadly developed *fugato* on a short theme built almost entirely on chromatic intervals). The scherzo (third movement) is a musical genre picture inspired largely by the carols sung in South Russia on Christmas Eve. There are also suggestions and *motifs* from Russian folk songs in the themes of the finale.

The folk element in all these themes led to a considerable change in the composer's technique. The texture of his music became more transparent, the harmonic language more simple, the instrumentation more colorful and—perhaps most important of all—the melodic line became more clearly defined.

Myaskovsky's mastery of the symphonic form is expressed here in the symmetrical construction of the work as a whole, the logical development of its themes and its organic integrity of form. In this respect each of the movements contains much that is of value and is worthy of close study. The first movement, for instance, shows a superb treatment of the problem of thematic transposition in the recapitulation in contrast to the exposition, which constitutes a brilliant digression from the usual pattern of the sonata allegro. The recapitulation is actually introduced during the development of the subordinate theme (which is the *first* to be repeated), but only makes itself felt with the subsequent repetition of the main theme. This has an extraordinary influence on the logical development of the musical ideas. The tranquil total effect of the movement is remarkably deepened by the dynamic and strenuous building up of the climax, and holds us in a spell with its implicit promise of inevitable development. The andante is built up of two finely contrasted musical ideas—one *tranquillo,* in cradle-song style; the other (the middle section—*fugato*) violent, like something that is chained and struggles to be free.

The scherzo gives utterance to the spirit of the dance. Its prevailing tone is gloomy with occasional flashes of color. This movement is notable for the masterly development of the two principal ideas (contrasting in color but similar in their dynamic quality), the monolithic unity of the whole and the brilliance of the instrumentation. The finale is bright and majestic, with a remarkable coda in which Myaskovsky builds up a grand climax of sound and movement, making masterly use of the broad, powerful melody of the subordinate theme of the first movement.

When asked if the Fifth Symphony bore any relation to the war of 1914–1917, Myaskovsky replied: "No direct relation at all. It would be much more appropriate to ask this about my Fourth Symphony, which ousted the Fifth Symphony that I had conceived much earlier; and yet even the relation of the Fourth Symphony to the war was more of a general psychological reaction than anything else. Actually the majority of the themes of the Fifth Symphony occurred to me during the war in the most varied circumstances, which were mostly peaceful enough, although in the zone of the front. The opening theme of the first movement came to me in a fir wood near the fort of Przemysl in 1915. The themes of the scherzo [9] originated near Dvinsk in 1916, while the themes of the finale came to me in urban surroundings in 1917, while I was at Revel." [10]

"The war considerably enriched my store of inner and

---

[9] Except for the second episode—the Christmas carols—which Myaskovsky heard in December, 1914, in the village of Sokolniki, near Lvov, Galicia.

[10] From a letter to the author, October 2, 1935.

external impressions and for some reason tended to brighten my musical ideas to a certain extent." [11]

At first glance it might seem paradoxical (as it seemed doubtless to the composer himself, when he used the phrase "for some reason") that the war and its horrors should have been conducive to "brightening his musical ideas." But, in actual fact, there is no paradox here. It would be a mistake to look for any direct reaction to the horrors of war in the Fifth Symphony or for a direct reflection of social events.[12] The influence of the war on Myaskovsky's work, and on his Fifth Symphony in particular, operated in an entirely different direction.

The war freed the composer from the comparatively restricted circle of feelings and interests which had dominated him until then. It was the broadening of his horizon, the establishment of a deeper contact between himself and the life of the people that infused such vitality into his musical ideas.

Symphony No. 6 in E-flat minor, Opus 23

The idea has taken root among music critics that Myaskovsky's Sixth Symphony expresses his attitude to the Revolution. Probably there is no other large work of Myaskovsky's

---

[11] "Autobiographical Notes."

[12] Inasmuch as this was the rôle of the Fourth Symphony, which was indeed written under the influence of the war as a direct "reflection" of what Myaskovsky "had just been through." The dramatic character of the music of the Fourth Symphony, its sharp dynamic upsurges, the peculiar acrid tones of the chromatic harmonies, all speak of the "revolts" from which the composer wanted to "relax" after the Second and Third Symphonies. In the Fourth Symphony, on the whole, Myaskovsky remains in his former sphere of thoughts and emotions.

that was "nursed" for so long. The first idea originated in 1919. The external circumstances of its creation was Myaskovsky's residence with the Derzhanovsky family, whose apartment was a sort of center for musicians, writers and the like.

On one occasion Derzhanovsky's circle was visited by an artist (his name has been lost) who had lived for some time in France and Italy. He told many stories of the life of the people in these countries, and in France particularly. He had often heard the workers and artisans of the Paris suburbs singing their favorite songs in the open air after their day's work, and gave the company a spirited rendering of the melody of the *Carmagnole*.

"This man made a deep impression on me," says Myaskovsky, "and I made up my mind to write a symphony expressing in some way the feelings that he had roused in me. The original and highly dynamic construction of the *Carmagnole* as sung by the artist greatly appealed to me and was quite unlike anything I had ever found in the usual editions (including all the most authoritative versions). Later, in the process of composition, I got the idea of including another song in the style of the *Carmagnole*. This was the *Ça Ira*, which I likewise treated in an entirely new way in my exposition and harmonization of the melody.

"I worked on the Sixth Symphony for a whole year. In the interval between the initial impulse (when I made the first sketch of the song) and the final realization of the plan an important part in the process of crystallization was played by a reading of Verhaeren's *Les Aubes*, which I also included in the framework of the symphony. *Les Aubes* became what might be called the pre-idea of the work: the death of a revolutionary hero and the solemn honors paid to him by the people in farewell. The symphony was completed only in 1923." [13]

The theory that the Sixth Symphony is associated with the memory of two of the composer's friends who are supposed to have perished in the Revolution is a fallacy.[14] The only fact which could have had any such bearing on his work was the death of his aunt, Yelikonida Konstantinovna Myaskovskaya, in the winter of 1920. This had some significance of a purely biographical character. The flat where Yelikonida Konstantinovna had lived was bleak, cheerless and very cold. The wind whistled and howled in the chimneys. All this left its mark on Myaskovsky when he returned to Petrograd— particularly the howling of the wind. "I wanted to include this impression in the scherzo. Of course, it had no bearing on the musical content of the symphony, except as a purely external impulse." [15]

The Sixth Symphony [16] is written in four movements. The first is a broadly developed allegro in sonata form, full of musical variety. A short, highly characteristic introduction of three imperative and exclamatory chords twice repeated *tutti, fortissimo* is followed by the sharply rhythmic, mobile and resilient theme of the opening subject. Then follows a troubled, somewhat sinister episode like a message of ill-boding in *tempo accelerando*. This passage is later supplemented by a new theme in the form of a fanfare. Gradually

[13] From a conversation with Myaskovsky.—A. I.
[14] Y. V. Keldysh's article, "Myaskovsky's 12th Symphony and Problems of Soviet Symphonism," *Sovietskaya Muzyka*, No. 2, 1934.
[15] From a conversation with Myaskovsky.—A. I.
[16] Myaskovsky's Sixth Symphony was performed for the first time on May 24, 1924, in Moscow by the orchestra and chorus of the State Academic Theatre, conducted by Nikolai Golovanov.

the general tension subsides and gives place to a second phase of moods: a contemplative solemn chorale, a few bars of flowing, languorous music, and finally the theme, woven of soft, sighing intonations suggestive of a subdued complaint, which brings the exposition to a close.

It might be said that throughout the first movement, no less than in the exposition, there are two kinds of musical ideas—those expressive of insistence, impetuosity and mobility and, in contrast to these, lyrical passages of vague, tender nature, the sublime, ethereal emotions of a mind immersed in elegiac dreams. This second group of ideas symbolizes the world of a man who has become detached from his real environment.

At the end of the first movement the effect of these moods is almost cataleptic in its intensity. The gloomy *tremolando* of the strings, the measured and dull booming of the bass drum in triplets, the descending progression of chords over a long-sustained tonic pedal point are all conducive to this effect.

In the second movement (*presto tenebroso*) the composer evidently set out to create an atmosphere of mystery and darkness and in this he is entirely successful. Although each of its themes is entirely distinctive, they all bear the common imprint of gloom as of some physical presence, a sense of "creepiness" such as might be evoked by the sound of a moaning wind or a blizzard out-of-doors. The whirling effect created by the different devices employed in the opening theme and the theme of the first subject, ranging from the lowest registers of the orchestra to the highest, the tonality, which is one of the most somber of the minor keys (F minor), the use of the augmented scale, the tenseness of tone of the melodic material due to the chromatic construction of the themes, the steady thud of the bass in the second theme, and finally the listless and melancholy murmur of the muted but sonorous strings with the *celesta* in the middle episode (musically akin to the lamentation of the maniac in Moussorgsky's *Boris Godounov*)—these are a few of the devices with which the composer conveys his ideas.

The third movement—*andante*—belongs essentially to the same sphere of musical ideas as the first movement, although with a difference which springs from a certain modification of the images expressing weariness, tenderness and, as it were, a renunciation of all excitement, unrest and "materiality." Occasionally there are threatening chords, like malignant flashes against this dark background, which recall vividly to mind the introduction to the symphony. These, however, are exceptions and do no more than interrupt for a brief period the prevailing mood of the movement.

The finale is a grand apotheosis of all that has gone before. At the same time the composer broaches new problems of expression and attains original solutions. The stormy, revolutionary *Carmagnole,* the categorical emphasis of the *Ça Ira,* the *Dies Irae* and a Russian folk song dealing with the parting of soul and body [17]—such are the *leitmotifs* of the finale. The composer superbly lays bare the essence of the *Ça Ira,* and *Carmagnole* as songs of the people and symbols of Revolution. From these he achieves a natural and sincere transition to the lament for the dead hero—the *Dies Irae* as a symbol of death and the aptly chosen theme of the Russian folk song. The idea of life and death is closely interwoven with the whole fabric of the symphony.

------

[17] Taken from the album *Old Songs of the Voronezh Province,* edited by M. S. Pyatnitsky.

It is only in the finale that the conflicting elements which are outlined in the first movement of the symphony, and are developed at length in the second and third movements, are finally placed and solved. The idea of life is interwoven with the idea of Revolution; the idea of death is interwoven with the inevitable sacrifices of the Revolution and the inevitable grief of bereavement. In this work Myaskovsky records in terms of symphonic music the attitude to the Revolution of a large section of the Russian intelligentsia, by whom it was fervently accepted but not as yet fully understood.

The artistic power of the Sixth Symphony, the depth of its ideas, secure for it a special place in Russian music. For force of generalization it can be compared only with the last symphony of Tchaikovsky. In this connection it should be pointed out that the Sixth Symphony was no chance offshoot of the composer's career. Its nearest prototype is perhaps the Third Symphony; but its deep roots go back to *Alastor,* and certain passages from *The Vow of Silence* in the sphere of symphonic music, and to the Second Sonata in F-sharp minor in Myaskovsky's works for the pianoforte. There is a world of difference between the Third and Sixth Symphonies, despite their kinship in color and movement. The essence of the Third Symphony lies in its expression of vague and troubled aspirations, culminating in tragedy, whereas the power of the Sixth Symphony lies in its reflection of a real struggle above personalities—its reflection of the Revolution in the creative consciousness of the composer.

Symphony No. 7 in B minor, Opus 24

While the Sixth Symphony was still in the stage of rough draft, Myaskovsky had already started work on a seventh symphony, which he soon finished and rounded off. Only after this did he return to the completion of the Sixth Symphony.

On the one hand, the Seventh Symphony shows signs of a certain relaxation of tension, as though the composer, in spite of himself, found his attention drawn to tranquil, "objective" images (cradle song, *musette*). On the other hand, in this symphony he dwells in a personal, intimate world of ideas in which the stormy power of the Sixth Symphony still finds an echo. This is not a question, of course, of mere textual repetition. What happened was that the same "subjective" emotions and images that had inspired the Sixth Symphony again sprang to life in the Seventh.

In tracing the development of Myaskovsky's art we notice more than once these echoes, or residual upsurges of inspiration, manifested in different forms.

Symphony No. 8 in A major, Opus 26

The Eighth Symphony was drafted in the summer of 1924. Here is what the composer himself has to say of its conception: "The symphony is about Stepan Razin. The first movement is an epic, a narrative, the steppes, Nature. The second movement is a scherzo, all the themes of which, except the novel first theme in 7/4 time (which I wrote while I was still a pupil of I. I. Kryzhanovsky about thirty years ago), are associated with 'water.' One is 'A Little Duck Swam on the Sea,' the other, 'Little Pike Fish'—both taken from Rimsky-Korsakov's collection. Both are in 7/4 time.

"The principal theme of the third movement symbolizes the distress of the peasantry. It is based on a Bashkirian folk melody to which people used to sing the words of the popular song about the lonely soldier's wife. In the middle of the third movement there is a brighter passage characterizing the girl in the legend—the Persian princess.[18] But it does not last long. The mood of sadness returns and the music goes back to the song about the soldier's wife.

"The last movement deals with the exploits of Stepan Razin and the coda represents his death. B. V. Krassin gave me the theme for the finale in 1921. I thought at the time that this was a theme associated with Razin, but such was not the case. I discovered later that it was from Balakirev. It was included as No. 9 in the album *Thirty Russian Songs,* arranged for four hands, under the title of *Grishka Otrepyev.* Forgetting that the theme was from Balakirev and the song about Grishka Otrepyev (although Krassin had told me exactly where he had got it from), I somehow took it into my head that it was associated with Razin and began to work out the symphony along these lines.[19]

We see that in this most interesting composition Myaskovsky draws upon folk *motifs* not only for his subject, but also in the strict musical sense. This was a fact of the greatest importance for his further development.

However, from the point of view of its style, the Eighth Symphony still revealed certain characteristic traits which tended to "befog" the composition as a whole: a tendency to tense, "astringent" harmonies and to extreme density in the musical texture, which is overburdened by the polyphonic treatment of the material. Add to this that Myaskovsky, far from expressing his ideas in simple pictures, strives continually to give them a deeper and more complex expression, and

---

[18] A captive of Stepan Razin. He threw her overboard as a gift to the River Volga.

[19] From a conversation with Myaskovsky.—A. I.

it will be understood that, although the symphony has a definite story as its background and contains an element of folklore, the music remains fairly abstruse.

Symphony No. 9 in E minor, Opus 28

The Eighth Symphony was finally orchestrated in 1925. On completing it Myaskovsky, just as after the Third and Sixth Symphonies, felt the need for some sort of relief from the tense strain of composition. It should never be forgotten that in Myaskovsky's work these moments of "residual discharge" and relaxation are highly significant. Without going into a detailed analysis of them we may safely say that they are an indispensable element of his creative development. After the "revolts" of the Second and Third Symphonies, Myaskovsky felt that he must write a "quiet" symphony (the Fifth). After the Sixth he felt the need to "let off steam" with the Seventh. In the same way he felt that he must write a sort of "symphonic intermezzo" after the Eighth. The result was the Ninth Symphony.

In comparison with its predecessors the Ninth Symphony has more of the romantic spirit. It has a certain dream-like quality, is lucid and lyrical in mood and transparent as regards the musical fabric. This tendency is most apparent in the first three movements.

The romanticism of this symphony lies not only in its ideas but also in its very form. In defiance of the accepted traditions of the classics, Myaskovsky bases the first movement of the symphony on a free development of the complex ternary form and uses the sonata allegro pattern for the second movement of the symphony, which is a scherzo.

In the andante (third movement),[20] which is unusually rich in thematic content, we are struck by the moving sincerity of the opening theme (solo clarinet), which is saturated with the spirit of the Russian folk song, and by the chill sullenness of the middle episode, which is given to the bass flute. In this movement there is also some very effective use of the brass in chorded episodes of symbolic significance, suggestive of oratory or declamation.[21]

This impression of oratory is heightened by the peculiar rhythm with pauses on the accented beats—a common device with Myaskovsky. In its constant efforts to bring out the full significance of each phrase the music may be compared with the natural inflections of human speech. Myaskovsky is especially skillful in the use of such rhythms with frequent employment of the brass.[22]

The finale is written in the composer's favorite form—the rondo. With the exception of its lucid classical first theme the finale is based almost entirely on thematic material taken from the first and second movements of the symphony. In spite of these thematic links with the earlier parts of the work, however, the finale is not convincing enough as a conclusion, and fails to round off the symphony. Myaskovsky himself regards this as the "least successful" movement of the four.

Symphony No. 10 in F minor, Opus 30

After this "symphonic intermezzo," which was framed "as nearly as possible in a spirit of untroubled lyricism," Myas-

---

[20] The third movement, like the first, is in three-part form.
[21] *Cf.* the transition from the first movement.
[22] See the chapter on *Musical Technique*, Example No. 15.

kovsky produced the acutely psychological and distraught
music of the Tenth Symphony. The central idea of the symphony is the mental anguish of Eugene in Pushkin's *Bronze
Horseman*.

While carefully following Pushkin's story in the composition of this symphony, Myaskovsky did not make it a program
piece in the strict sense of the term. He entirely omits the
scene of the flood in St. Petersburg and in general shuns all
pictorial elements. The symphony has a different aim—that
of presenting a psychological study of its heroes.

The principal idea of the symphony is taken from the well-
known illustration by Alexander Benois to Pushkin's *Bronze
Horseman*, which shows Eugene fleeing in horror from his
pursuer—Falconet's equestrian statue of Peter the Great.

There are three images in the symphony—Eugene himself,
his wife Parasha and Peter's monument—the Bronze Horseman.

The Tenth Symphony has affinities with the tone poem
Alastor. In *Alastor* the composer's attention is concentrated on
the central figure of his work, while he relegates the image of
Alastor's vision to a secondary place. So, too, the central idea
of the Tenth Symphony is the distraction of Eugene, while
the theme of Parasha remains brief and episodic. It is characteristic of Myaskovsky that the Tenth Symphony is at the
same time a culmination of those exhausting harmonic and
melodic searchings through which he had passed.

Perhaps it should be pointed out here, in connection with
Myaskovsky's Tenth Symphony, that, whereas he respects
and draws freely on the musical traditions of the past, he is
no slave to dogma. He thinks in terms of contemporary music,
constantly seeking for new content and discovering new
forms of expressing it.

Generally speaking, it may be said that Myaskovsky's music has the quality of expressiveness to a high degree. This quality, too, is especially conspicuous in the Tenth Symphony. Myaskovsky employs here the devices of the German school of expressionism or, to be more specific, the devices of its most gifted representative—Arnold Schönberg. All three themes in the symphony—Eugene, the Bronze Horseman and Parasha —are built on ten semitones of the chromatic scale. These ten semitones are used not only as passing notes but as fundamental notes, thus determining both the melodic patterns of the symphony and the harmonic fabric, to which they impart a poignant, haunting quality. In spite of all the refinement and complexity of Myaskovsky's technique, the music is tense and urgent, and the whole work, with its powerful representation of a human mind in turmoil, is strikingly dramatic.

Miscellaneous Works, 1927–1931

"While I was engaged on the Tenth Symphony," [23] writes Myaskovsky, "which cost me some effort, I got the idea of writing a series of orchestral suites in song and dance idioms. The thematic material of all three took shape suddenly, 'at one sitting.' Not long afterwards came Opus 32, consisting of a *Serenade* for small orchestra, a *Sinfonietta* for string orchestra (this gained rather wide popularity, particularly abroad), and a *Lyrical Concertino* for mixed ensemble. In these three-part suites my original plan underwent certain changes and the dance element unfortunately failed to receive

---

[23] The Tenth Symphony was written simultaneously with the Ninth in 1926–1927.

proper expression, but I did, nevertheless, manage to achieve greater clarity than formerly in the flow of ideas and their treatment." [24]

The principal merit of the three orchestral suites which the composer grouped under a single opus number (what a store of creative energy must have been his if the entire thematic material, that is, at least twenty themes, occurred to him "at one sitting!") is unquestionably the profoundly national Russian character of the music. All the suites are "caressing" in tone (to use the expression of B. V. Asafyev) and reveal an emotional sincerity which is typically Russian, and which is at once reminiscent of Tchaikovsky and Moussorgsky.

Four years passed between the composition of the 10th and 11th Symphonies (1927–1931). In this interval, Myaskovsky wrote only Opus 32 in the symphonic genre. Besides Opus 32 he wrote two quartets, which he grouped together under Opus 33, and a new version of his early quartet in D minor. During the same period he re-edited and combined in two volumes his earlier pieces (*Frolics*) for the pianoforte under the title of *Reminiscences* and *Yellowed Leaves*. He also broke fresh ground with two marches for military band and a number of popular songs.

This period was highly important in the creative development of the composer. In it we see a growing urge to respond in musical terms to the demands of life and modern society. It was a period of acute ideological conflict in the musical world, a period of revision of values, a time when composers had to take a definite stand on the question of the classical tradition, musical genres and the ideological content of art.

---

[24] "Autobiographical Notes."

Symphony No. 11 in B-flat minor, Opus 34, and Symphony No. 12 in G minor, Opus 35

Myaskovsky was profoundly stirred by the problem of the creation of symphonic works reflecting the ideological and esthetic trends of our day. The whole history of the composition of the Sixth Symphony (the orchestration of the French revolutionary songs, Verhaeren's *Les Aubes*), the conception of the Eighth Symphony, the idea of Opus 32 (works in the song and dance idiom), the so-called lyrical "intermezzo"— the Ninth Symphony—were all fruit of the intense creative energy of a deep-thinking Soviet artist, aimed in a single direction.

"When the first calls were made for the collectivization of peasant farming this idea greatly fascinated me and I believed it would be particularly revolutionary in its results. One day M. Koval at a conference held under the auspices of the State Publishing House of Music gave me a hint for the subject of a musical composition to depict the spring sowing. Almost immediately I conceived the musical ideas and general plan for a symphony about the countryside, showing it before the new life, in the struggle for this new life and during the new life. In the autumn of 1931 I got down to the task in real earnest, but first of all I managed to write my 11th Symphony in which I gave outlet to more subjective moods." [25]

From this statement it is clear that the 11th Symphony, as an expression of the composer's personal emotions, was easier to compose than the programmatic 12th Symphony.

It is a current opinion that when Myaskovsky regards any

---

[25] *Ibid.*

of his works as a reflection of his own subjective feelings, the work in question is always highly characteristic in its technique and somewhat one-sided in its range of ideas. Actually, however, despite its predominant use of the compound (or augmented) scale,[26] the complexity of its harmonies and the polyphonic treatment of its thematic material, the music of the 11th Symphony is lucid and coherent in mood, recalling rather the works of Borodin or Moussorgsky than, say, recherché music of Scriabin.

In the same flow of inspiration that engendered the 11th Symphony Myaskovsky also wrote the 12th Symphony, which was dedicated to the Fifteenth Anniversary of the Great October Socialist Revolution. The latter work was the subject of many articles in the Soviet press and created a considerable stir in the musical circles of Moscow.

In this work Myaskovsky attempted to do justice in large symphonic form to a mighty factor of Socialist culture—the collectivization of the farms, expressed, as he puts it, in images of the countryside "before the new life, in the struggle for this new life, and during the new life." But the task he had set himself proved too imposing. The musical themes of the symphony fell short of its subject. Thus the work suffers from a "lack of contagious and fascinating melodic directness —an inadequate 'vocalization' of ideas." [27] These words of the composer, although they were spoken in reference to his songs, might be applied equally well to some of his larger works and in particular to the 12th Symphony. The music does not take sufficient hold on the imagination, and the symphony contains features of abstract rationalistic thought,

---

[26] For instance, in the development of the first movement, in the treatment of the middle portion of the andante (*fugato*), and in the coda of the finale.

[27] "Autobiographical Notes."

which detract from the vividness and directness of the music.

Yet in spite of these shortcomings the historical significance of the 12th Symphony as an important step in the development of Soviet symphonic music is not to be underestimated. It was the first attempt in the symphonic form to express the broad aspects of Soviet life in major, realistic works of art.

Symphony No. 13 in B-flat minor, Opus 36

This symphony (in one movement) was written during an illness at the end of 1933 (two years after the 12th). To use the composer's own expression, it was conceived "at one stroke," [28] in a sudden fit of inspiration which came to him one night when he could not go to sleep because of his high temperature. It was first performed in Chicago in 1934 by the Philharmonic Orchestra conducted by Frederick Stock. In the Soviet Union it was rendered by the Radio Committee orchestra conducted by Leo Ginsburg.

The music of the 13th Symphony moves through a comparatively narrow circle of moods "strange in the extreme," [29] woven of a despondency and spiritual desolation verging on stupor and punctuated with sudden emotional rises and falls, the exact psychological basis of which is hard to determine.

Myaskovsky himself calls the 13th Symphony "pages from a diary," and describes the music as "pessimistic" and "strange." [30] And there is every reason for assuming that the subjective feeling which gave rise to this work was induced to some extent by the composer's dissatisfaction with his pre-

---

[28] *Ibid.*   [29] *Ibid.*   [30] *Ibid.*

ceding work (the 12th Symphony, his first large-scale musical
essay on a Soviet theme) [31] and the heavy strain which it
cost him.

Symphony No. 14 in C major, Opus 37

In the 14th Symphony, in five parts, written in 1933,
Myaskovsky made something of a departure from the traditional symphonic form, but at the same time did not make
such a break as could be regarded as new in principle. The
first, third, and fifth movements are quick, while the second
and fourth are slow movements.

The music of the second movement—*andantino*—differs
somewhat in character from movements of this kind in other
symphonies. Its first and last sections are in *cantabile* style and
lyrical in tone, leaving an impression of inner tranquillity.
The melody flows gently, makes easy hearing and its repeti-
tions cause no fatigue. It has that peculiar folk-song quality
by which, however often the *motif* is repeated, it never wearies
or cloys. The middle episode of the *andantino* consists of
variations on a quick-moving theme of Kazakh origin.

The uninterrupted panoramic effect of the whole movement gives it a place of its own among the rest of Myaskovsky's slow movements. It is a sort of musical genre picture
beginning and ending on a lyrical note with the dance idiom
prevailing in the middle portion. The *andantino* also marks
a stage in Myaskovsky's development as a whole. From the
time of the 14th Symphony onward the dominant urge of the

---

[31] "The 12th Symphony did not work out quite as I intended; it was
schematic in places, but the main thing was that I could not find the required
idiom and form for the last movement, which thus expressed my ideas outwardly but inwardly lacked conviction." ("Autobiographical Notes.")

composer was to compose music with a tranquil "pulse of life," music with clear ideas and a simple language.

Symphony No. 15 in D minor, Opus 38

Myaskovsky's 15th Symphony belongs to this same prolific period. It was composed in 1933–1934, and is in four movements, and continues the same line as the 14th. "I tussled with it for a whole year," said Myaskovsky. "I worked for six months on the fifth bar of the andante. All my versions were too intricate. The theme itself was simple, and I was seeking simplicity." [32]

The 15th Symphony is luminous and joyful. This is especially true of the principal themes of the first and fourth movements. Both are spirited and vigorous and yet gentle with an undertone of serenity.

The second movement, a lyrical andante, is notable for its warm feeling, transparency of mood and clear construction. At the same time it is not free from stern and somewhat gloomy moments suggested by the composer's favorite orchestral devices (chord successions in the lower register rendered by the brass, often in combination with the clarinets and bassoons).

The third movement, scherzo, is superficially reminiscent of the delicacy and lightness of Tchaikovsky's waltzes, although there are moments when the waltz features are eclipsed by the symphonic development of the music. The waltz gives the symphony an added vivacity and a more direct appeal, making it less abstract. This apparent intrusion of a "low-brow" musical form into so dignified a work as a

---

[32] From a conversation with Myaskovsky.—A. I.

symphony was no accident. On the contrary, it must be regarded as one of the symphony's peculiar bridges to realism.

The work ends in a festive and joyous finale.

The 15th Symphony has much in common with the Fifth, to which it bears a significant resemblance in its tonal plan— D minor (first movement), B minor (second movement), G minor (third movement), D minor (fourth movement) [33]— and the use of the dance idiom in the scherzo. In general, the 15th Symphony is more lyrical, more warm and transparent than the Fifth. It is a rich and joyous page in the career of Myaskovsky.

Symphony No. 16 in F major, Opus 39

On October 24, 1936, an audience in the Great Hall of the Moscow Conservatory heard the first performance of Myaskovsky's 16th Symphony (in four movements) conducted by Szenkar. This new work was an immediate success, and the composer was given an ovation. It is possible that this favorable reaction was partly prepared for by the warm reception accorded the 15th Symphony. But to a large extent it was undoubtedly due to the appealing melodic line of the symphony's themes. The melodies are so sustained that the ear effortlessly memorizes their outline and character and is fully satisfied by the music. In this respect the 16th Symphony is superior to many of Myaskovsky's earlier symphonic works, whose melodies are fragmentary and incoherent, and fail to satisfy.

In certain passages of the symphony the exposition of the melody assumes a broad, developed form (binary) with an

---

[33] Although in the Fifth Symphony the first and the last movements are major.

expressiveness that reminds us of the *romanza* or "song without words." This is true, for instance, of the first theme of the second movement, and it is true of the concluding section of the finale. It can confidently be stated that the chief resource of musical expression in the 16th Symphony is melody. This trait is extremely important not only in regard to the essential beauty which it imparts to the 16th Symphony itself, but because in later works—the 17th and 21st Symphonies, the Violin Concerto, the romances—this becomes a dominant feature of Myaskovsky's style.

Virtually every melody of the 16th Symphony bears its own hallmark. The precipitant character of the main theme of the allegro is due to its rising melodic flow no less than to its rhythm. The diatonic progressions in the natural scale and the sustained phrases of the second theme give it the coloring of a folk song, restrained, austere and pure in its simplicity. In the charming intermezzo the ear readily picks out the elegant pattern of the theme in the Italian *arioso* style. The following subjects are light and rhythmic. The finely molded *motif* of the march evokes the picture of a funeral cortège and one of its melodies (in descending progression), in which tenderness is blended with grief, is particularly striking. The finale is a mine of thematic variety.

The first movement, *allegro vivace,* vibrates with action. The opening theme carries the listener away with an irresistible impetuosity which is checked only by the second theme, that immediately restores tranquillity with its warmly lyrical, singing tones. Subsequently, the second theme catches some of the fire and dynamic quality of the first theme and, as the music develops, becomes enriched with these new characteristics.

The general lucidness of the allegro is largely due to the

laconic treatment of its thematic material and to its simplicity of form.

The images of the second movement are profoundly lyrical. The first theme, *andantino,* in the style of a cantilena, is contemplative and vivacious by turns. It seems to be woven from the very stuff of Nature. The gay *musette* and the snatches of song-like melody that answer it are genuine folk *motifs* which the composer noted down in the countryside near Moscow in 1932 and 1933.

The third movement (*andante*) is a funeral march. It records the profound sensations of the composer on learning of the tragic disaster which overtook the giant plane *Maxim Gorky* in 1935.

The modal peculiarities of the first theme of the march, which impart major intonations to a minor key, the unbroken melodic development of the theme itself, the precise march rhythm and the logical sequence of the music from culmination to culmination—all these combine to create a general impression of fortitude and reserve. The march is dramatic, but not despairing, although in the middle section the composer seems to give free rein to a deep and genuine sorrow. Into this almost unbroken general mood of solemn resolve Myaskovsky infuses a peculiarly warm and human tone with his occasional lyrical digressions. In the march as a whole he seems to strike a synthesis of austerity and sorrow, courage and tenderness. The music loses a little by being somewhat drawn out.

The principal theme of the finale is the aviators' song (*Planes are Flying*) in *moderato* tempo, *cantabile* style, but with an upward surge. The second and fourth themes are all but dance pieces. The finale closes with a lyrical melody.

The 16th Symphony has no program and needs none. It is

a musical epitome of moods and sentiments of the people of our time. The broad song-like finale, a poem of purpose, heroism, love of nature, the power of life triumphant and the bitterness of bereavement, summarizes, as it were, the varied moods of the other movements.

Symphony No. 17 in G-sharp minor, Opus 41

The 17th Symphony (in four parts) was written in 1936–1937. Here is a full flood of human emotion. The 17th Symphony is sheer song from first to last. In the imperative and clear melody of the main theme of the first movement Myaskovsky attains remarkable clarity of rhythm and outline. The very character of the music, swelling from *piano* to *forte* and consistently and impetuously gaining momentum, declares this to be the first movement. This theme, with its laconic phrasing and finely chiseled contours, is succeeded by the deep, translucent, flowing *cantabile* of the second theme, which is "one of the most convincing and clear melodies which our composers have written in recent years." [34]

The second movement is characterized by its colorful main theme, a lilting *andantino,* beautifully brought out by the strings, especially where they are augmented by the harp and clarinet. The lyrical, haunting melody of this theme with its recitative passages and sustained harmonic accompaniment, gives it a tender and, at the same time, dramatic tone and lends the music an added poignancy.

The third movement (scherzo) is a filigree casket, if we may use the expression, of original themes in the authentic Russian spirit, now resilient and march-like in character, now

---

[34] G. Neuhaus, "The 17th Symphony of Myaskovsky." *Sovietskoye Iskusstvo,* No. 1, 1938.

reminiscent of the song and dance idioms. And, lastly, the
dominating theme of the finale is in the tradition of Tchaikovsky's broad, rich melodies. This latter theme derives a special
charm from its broad diapason, its bright harmonies in major
tone, the smooth flow of its melody and the ascending line of
its pattern, which rises in two successive waves. Equally note-
worthy is the brilliant and dynamic music of the *fugato* in the
finale. Here the polyphonic form (fugue), welded with the
rest of the movement into one organic whole, is molded with
rare plasticity and clarity of thought.

The prevailing tone of the 17th Symphony is bright,
dynamic and profoundly emotional. Moreover—and this is
one of the main reasons why the music is so convincing—it
reflects with unmistakable emphasis the original, individual
features of Myaskovsky's style.

Symphony No. 18 in C major, Opus 42

The 18th Symphony was dedicated to the Twentieth
Anniversary of the Great October Socialist Revolution. It
was composed in the summer of 1937 and orchestrated in
September of the same year.

The 18th Symphony is Opus 32 on a new plane. The song
and dance idiom, the essentially Russian character of the
themes, exceptional clarity in the flow of ideas and their
treatment—these features are even more prominent in the
18th Symphony than in Opus 32, which was written almost
ten years earlier.

From the point of view of formal structure alone, the 18th
Symphony (in three movements, the first and last of which
are in quick tempo, while the middle movement is slow)
seems to re-echo the three-movement suites of Opus 32. This

resemblance is particularly striking with regard to the *Lyrical Concertino* (Op. 32, No. 3).

The main idea which prompted the composer to write Opus 32, but which, according to his own confession, failed to receive adequate development at the time, now found convincing expression in his 18th Symphony. The composer's persistent search for musical resources which would make a large orchestral work more appealing to the masses led him in his work to draw lavishly on the song and dance idiom.

This is borne out by a remark which Myaskovsky made not long before writing the 18th Symphony. He first gave the following brief characterization of the symphony: "For the Twentieth Anniversary of the October Revolution I was planning a rather ambitious piece for orchestra and chorus." [35] Then referring to this new project in a subsequent conversation with the author, he added: "I wanted to write some popular songs. But I had no text, so they came out as songs without words—the themes of the 18th Symphony." In other words, the musical media which the composer had particularly in mind when he planned the 18th Symphony, were those of song and dance.

A year after its composition Myaskovsky received from Professor A. A. Alschvang a letter with an enclosure from a peasant named Sergei Ivanovich Korsakov. Alschvang wrote: "Living in the countryside, Korsakov has developed a passion for music, listens avidly and, as a man of some gifts, he expresses fresher and more profound opinions than many of our would-be pundits. In this letter he offers an interesting appreciation of your 18th Symphony. I think that this favor-

---

[35] "Autobiographical Notes."

able comment of a man of the people will be of interest to you."

Here is an extract from Korsakov's letter:

"Recently I have fallen head over heels in love with some new productions and the first among them is Myaskovsky's 18th Symphony. I simply can't tell you how much I enjoy it. It's so full of vim and gusto, and brimful of good spirits. Especially in the first movement. There's a particularly fine passage there, you know, which is repeated three or four times, and occurs again in the finale. Of course, you can guess which passage I mean. I also like the second movement. Full of serene meditation, as though thinking about something good. The last musical phrase is especially impressive with its proud, majestic air. And then the third movement, which is full of folk-song themes, *Katya's Husband, the Ne'er-do-well* . . . and *The Crane,* and then one that I don't quite recognize, something in the style of a dance tune.[36] This symphony has so fascinated me that I don't know which movement is the best. That particular passage from the first movement is in my ears all the time."

Symphony No. 19 in E-flat major, Opus 46

In 1939 Myaskovsky wrote his 19th Symphony for military band, dedicated to the Twenty-first Anniversary of the Red Army. "At first the difficulties of this unusual task oppressed and discouraged me but I was anxious to keep my promise [37] and soon mustered a fair spurt of energy, with the

---

[36] These references to folk songs should be understood simply as the subjective musical associations of Korsakov, since the songs do not actually occur in the symphony itself.

[37] This was a promise given at the end of 1938 to an army bandmaster, I. V. Petrov, to write something for military band.

result that instead of a simple piece in one movement I was able to make the draft of a complete symphony in four movements. It turned out to be one of my more optimistic pieces. Its first and last movements are urgent and positive, while the middle movements take the form of a symphonized waltz (second movement) and a meditative *andante* (third movement)." [38]

This task of writing music "equally appreciable to experts and to the general public" for the limited ensemble of a cavalry unit military band proved to be one of extraordinary difficulty. Nevertheless, the 19th Symphony, which was begun on January 5, 1939, was finished in pianoforte score by January 13, and in the short space of time between the 15th and the 26th Myaskovsky finished the orchestration.

Violin Concerto in D minor, Opus 44

In the interval between the 18th and 19th Symphonies, Myaskovsky broke new ground with a three-movement concerto for violin and orchestra. This so far remains his first essay in this genre.

It is interesting to note the author's attitude to this work while he was composing it. He pursued two main aims: to create something "technically interesting for a virtuoso which, firstly, could be played with enjoyment and, secondly, should be easy for the audience." [39] In planning this concerto Myaskovsky looked virtually through the whole violin repertory in search of form, especially for the first movement. "The first movement did not come easily, because I was grappling

---

[38] From the Moscow Conservatory journal *Sovietsky Muzykant* [Soviet Musician], No. 45, 1939. "Myaskovsky on His Latest Symphony."

[39] From a conversation with Myaskovsky.—A. I.

here with a form quite new to me. I was anxious to combine the convenience of the performer with the required 'concert' effect in the exposition of material. At the same time I had to bear in mind the general musical quality of the whole. The first movement was written in three months, while the second movement was completed in two days and the finale in four." [40] Thus, Myaskovsky began the concerto in the middle of March, 1938, and finished it by the middle of June.

The first performer of the concerto, Professor David Oistrakh, gave his opinion of the work as follows: "The extraordinarily profound content of the concerto is combined with a remarkable exploitation of the violin's resources. Thanks to the essentially violinistic character of the work it is easily mastered and I am studying it without effort. In general, my work on this concerto is giving me a lot of satisfaction and enjoyment."

The main theme of the first movement, while entirely individual, continues and develops the characteristic features of the short, challenging orchestral introduction with which the concerto begins. In it tenderness is combined with masculinity, grace with nobility, mildness with resolution. The broad spontaneous melody of the second theme has a pathos reminiscent of Liszt and Tchaikovsky. The entire first movement of the concerto is strictly symphonic and is devoid of all pictorial elements. The *cadenza* which is almost an independent piece, touching upon all the themes of the first movement, brilliantly summarizes the emotional content of the movement as a whole.

The tranquil lyricism of the second movement (*adagio*) is in striking contrast to the tense drama of the first move-

---

[40] Y. Rabinovich and Y. Targonsky, "A Major Event." *Sovietsky Muzykant*, No. 10/25, 1938.

ment. The steadily ascending progressions of the melody (reminiscent of Liszt) express a mood of concentrated calm, followed (in the middle section) by a kind of musical water color in which the most subtle shades of thought and feeling find expression. The movement closes with a soaring melody which becomes gradually rarefied and is brightened at the end by a transition from minor to major.

The finale is based on song and dance themes, the first of which is particularly rich in the musical "finery" that is so well suited to the violin. The second is more intimate, with a marked *cantabile* quality, but although it is in a minor key it is spirited rather than melancholy. The third theme—in waltz style—is lyrical.

The outstanding merit of Myaskovsky's concerto is its symphonic quality. This is perhaps the most vital element of the whole work. In spite of certain unevennesses the different sections of the concerto are united by one idea, by a remarkable singleness of style and mood. This concerto is in essence a symphony for violin and orchestra, and a direct successor of the 18th Symphony.

Symphony No. 20 in E major, Opus 50, and Symphony No. 21 in F-sharp minor, Opus 51

Toward the end of March, or perhaps it was early in April, 1940, the Musical Department of the All-Union Radio Committee commissioned Myaskovsky to write a new symphonic production. This resulted in the 20th Symphony, in three movements, which was drafted between April 17 and May 23, and was orchestrated in September of the same year. Then on May 28 Myaskovsky started his 21st Symphony (in one movement) and completed it after twelve days' work.

At the Fourth Ten-day Festival of Soviet Music both these works were performed for the first time by the State Symphony Orchestra of the U.S.S.R., conducted by Alexander Hauck (21st Symphony) and the orchestra of the All-Union Radio Committee, conducted by Nikolai Golovanov (20th Symphony). These twin symphonies, though outwardly highly dissimilar, have a common sense of reality, common feeling for the life and moods of contemporary Soviet society.

*   *   *

Myaskovsky has been working for many years with exceptional persistence and success, writing music (especially in the symphonic genre) the ideas and language of which should express our epoch more vividly, reflect more readily its predominant feelings and moods and assert a positive attitude to life. With varying degrees of artistic force, in different forms yet always in his original manner, Myaskovsky gives expression to this ideal.

The symphonies themselves are extremely varied. The folk song and dance are the basis of the 18th Symphony. The highly concentrated and lyrical 21st Symphony, on the other hand, is a revelation of deep intimate feelings addressed to the outside world. The bright and somewhat ingenuous 14th Symphony, with its charming dance suggestions, seems to bear little resemblance to the broad, heroic lyricism of the 16th Symphony, or to the spontaneous and exuberant emotion of the 17th. The 15th Symphony, too, which, for all its peculiarly manful tone, is profoundly lyrical, stands in a category of its own.

Yet, in spite of the markedly individual character of these symphonies, they have a general common basis. This fundamental unity of Myaskovsky's work may perhaps be best illustrated by these typical appraisals from different musical critics of the following symphonies:

I. Ryzhkin, on the 16th Symphony: "Permeated with a true folk spirit . . . it is optimistic even in the tragic images of the slow movement." (*Sovietskoye Iskusstvo*, No. 49, October 27, 1937. "Myaskovsky and Soviet Symphony Music.")

G. Neuhaus, on the 17th Symphony: "This symphony seems to depict the emancipation and self-expression of the individual in our great epoch." (*Sovietskoye Iskusstvo*, No. 1, 1938.)

D. Kabalevsky, on the 18th Symphony: "The bright optimism of the first and third movements and the lyrical warmth of the second vividly express the world outlook of Soviet man." (*Molodaya Gvardia* [Young Guard].)

*   *   *

Myaskovsky's 20th Symphony, which in respect of its content and musical ideas follows in a direct line from his earlier works, might be described in analogous terms.

In its general coloring the first movement of the 20th Symphony is reminiscent of the first movement of the Violin Concerto. The subordinate theme of the first movement, indeed, with its flowing, undulating melody, was originally planned as the second theme of the Violin Concerto. The second movement (*adagio*) of the 20th Symphony, by reason of its content and, particularly, of its lovely orchestral effects, belongs unquestionably to the best pages of Myaskovsky's music. The *adagio* is a movement of epic calm (first theme) and smiling serenity (second theme). The finale recalls the first movement, but is more energetic and impetuous. One of its most memorable passages (subordinate theme) is an

authentic Ukrainian melody. The symphony closes with a
coda in E major, a whirlwind of sound effected with the full
power of the orchestra *tutti*.

Studied as a landmark in the career of Myaskovsky the
20th Symphony did not so much put forward new ideas or
open new horizons as consolidate and affirm trends which had
already made their appearance in his music.

Symphony No. 21 in F-sharp minor, Opus 51

The 21st Symphony (in one movement) was well received
by Moscow musical circles at its preliminary hearing held
under the auspices of the Union of Soviet Composers. It was
chosen to open the Ten-day Festival of Soviet Music (December, 1940), and has been subsequently included in numerous
symphony concerts.

The content and form of this composition are easily
grasped upon first acquaintance. It creates the impression of
being in three movements. The lengthy introduction (47
bars) in F-sharp minor, *andante sostenuto,* is accepted as a
single idea although it actually consists of two themes. This
introduction is written in a mood of profound meditation. It
is followed by the usual sonata allegro, a new section of considerable length which contains the exposition and development of two different themes: one impetuous with sharp
rhythms and syncopations (main theme, A minor); and the
other on an exalted lyrical plane, with a broad flowing
melody (subordinate theme, C major). The recapitulation
(D major) leads naturally to the concluding and third portion
of the symphony (F-sharp minor) which, with slight changes,
repeats the introduction. Such, in general terms, is the structure of Myaskovsky's 21st Symphony.

The masterly development of the thematic material, the harmonic and modal clarity of the music, the purity of the orchestration and the natural and logical flow of ideas wrought to a high pitch of expression make the 21st Symphony readily accessible to all and, as it were, a model in its genre. The emotional essence of a great work of art is too deep to be completely encompassed by such narrow definitions as "sad," "bright," "joyous," etc. In the same way the 21st Symphony is a work which transcends such conceptions.

Thus it may not be altogether by chance that the musical images of the 21st Symphony evoke associations with a whole series of Myaskovsky's earlier symphonies, compositions which stand poles apart in their emotional and ideological content.[41]

At the same time, it is one of the outstanding merits of the 21st Symphony that, notwithstanding the highly individual character of each of its *motifs,* the thematic material as a whole has that essential unity which reveals the hand of a master.

Here too are united stylistic traits typical both of Myaskovsky's earlier and later works. Here are the typical devices of polyphony so frequently met with in his music, the harmonies arising "incidentally" as a result of the independent movement of the parts—with all their multisonality—and the chromatic motion of the voices.

The 21st Symphony is written in one movement. Yet, with its remarkable unity of form and content, it reveals all

[41] *Cf.* the opening theme of the introduction (clarinet solo) with the clarinet solo in the main theme of the first movement of the 12th Symphony; the second theme of the introduction and the *fugato* of the 13th Symphony; the main theme of the sonata allegro with that of the first movement of the 15th Symphony, and the subordinate theme of the sonata allegro with that of the first movement of the 17th Symphony.

that unmistakable scope and breadth which is the hallmark
of the true *symphony*.

CHAMBER MUSIC, SONGS AND PIANOFORTE WORKS

Myaskovsky has worked prolifically not only in the symphonic field. He has written seven string quartets (including the F major quartet written in 1907, which has not been
published); over a hundred romances and songs; about the
same number of pieces for the piano, including six sonatas
left (four of them published); a sonata for violon-cello and
pianoforte, and a number of compositions for chorus, military
band, etc.

Perhaps the best known of these works at the present time
are Myaskovsky's quartets. Here, too, the composer gives
full play to his outstanding talents, to his constant tendency
to think in instrumental terms and his masterly symphonic
technique. A firm grasp of form, a sense of style, a strong and
unmistakable individuality and significance of content—these
are the main features of Myaskovsky's chamber music.

Apart from the unpublished quartet (which was the first
in order of composition) the quartets in F minor, Opus 33,
No. 4, and D minor, Opus 33, No. 3, are among his early
compositions. They were written in the composer's last two
years at the Conservatory (1909–1911).[1]

The F minor quartet is in four movements: allegro with
a short, slow introduction and coda; a scherzo (*allegro riso-*

---

[1] These two quartets were included in Opus 33 in 1930, after the composer
had completed the first two quartets of the group—No. 1 in A minor and
No. 2 in C minor.

luto); andante, and finale (*allegro molto*). The music is lucid, simple and sonorous. Unlike the other quartets grouped under the same opus number it avoids excessively jarring harmonies and intricate weavings of polyphony. Stable in tone and clear in melody, the F minor quartet leaves an impression of sincere emotion. It is both lyric and dramatic. The composer himself has expressed his dissatisfaction with this work, which he regards as too "emotional." Among the weak points of this quartet the critics have noted the lack of character in certain themes.

As played by leading Soviet ensembles, such as the Komitas, the Beethoven and the Bolshoi Theatre Quartets, the F minor quartet, for all its differences of interpretation, is characterized by the same spirit of romantic unrest and lyrical passion unadulterated by sentimentality. The fact that, from the point of view of its technique, this quartet is in some respects not so novel and original as the composer would have wished, does not obscure its unquestionable artistic merits.

The D minor quartet, Opus 33, No. 3 (in two parts), contains a joke at the expense of Lyadov, under whom Myaskovsky studied at the Conservatory in the class of free composition. Lyadov was a man of extraordinarily wide musical culture and an extremely critical approach. This explained, perhaps, his severity not only to himself and his pupils, but even to the great names of music. For instance, he disliked Grieg who, in his opinion, was guilty of a superabundance of thematic material and of irrationality and waste in using and developing it.

During his lessons in analysis of composition Lyadov sometimes made disparaging remarks about Grieg. In retaliation Myaskovsky wrote a quartet in which the opening theme of the first movement spelled the name Edvard Grieg (of course, not exactly) (Figure 1). The subordinate theme of the first

Figure 1. From the D minor quartet, Opus 33, No. 3
(opening theme).

movement was still more clearly provocative: "Beware of Lyadov!" (Figure 2). Furthermore, Myaskovsky utilized a

Figure 2. From the D minor quartet, Opus 33, No. 3
(subordinate theme).

genuine Grieg melody for the variations in the second movement of the quartet.

When he looked through the work, however, Lyadov did not notice the allusions and signified his approval.

While this quartet is not characteristic of the composer's style in general, Myaskovsky brilliantly passed in it his preliminary examination in the technique of chamber music. In the first movement the composer makes free and effective use of the sonata allegro pattern. After a short, logical development, rising to a clear culmination, he begins the recapitulation directly with the second theme, while the first theme is not repeated. The second movement includes some excellent variations (in E flat minor, a major and the concluding variations in D minor, which is a spirited and impetuous fugue). The harmonic language of the quartet is very clear and almost popular in conception.

During this same period Myaskovsky wrote his only Sonata for Violoncello and Piano. The sonata, Opus 12, is in two movements and is stylistically related to the E minor and D major quartets.

Twenty years later, in 1929–1930, Myaskovsky again turned his attention to chamber music and in a remarkably short space of time wrote two more quartets: Opus 33, No. 1 (A minor), and Opus 33, No. 2 (C minor).

The difference of style between these two quartets (especially the A minor quartet) and the composer's earlier works in this genre is somewhat the same as that between, for example, the Seventh, Eighth and Tenth, and the First Symphonies.

The quartet in A minor, which is in four movements, is extremely characteristic of the period when Myaskovsky was absorbed, above all, in seeking increasingly refined and intricate modes of expression.

At this time Myaskovsky's thought constantly turned to polyphony for a solution to the problems of musical expression. But he was not satisfied with the conventional devices of counterpoint as a means for developing his ideas. He strove constantly to achieve a genuinely free treatment of the voices and to grasp the functional chain of a musical theme not merely within the space of a few chords, but throughout large musical structures.

This had a marked effect on his handling of harmony.

Without breaking with the principle of tonic and dominant, Myaskovsky began to shape his harmonies not so much vertically as horizontally. He tended to limit his clear tonal statements to a series of "stepping stones" or "pivotal points." At the same time he developed the individual voices on the broadest possible lines, thus producing a number of "accidental" harmonic combinations or "collisions," which were resolved only as a result of tortuous wanderings.

The A minor quartet is extremely typical of this period of Myaskovsky. The predominant atmosphere of the first movement (sonata allegro) is one of suspense and instability. The recherché but unmelodious themes, the intricate weavings of the musical tissue, the sparsity of "points of rest," the dynamic rises and falls, all evoke a sense of strain and fatigue in the listener.

The scherzo (second movement), in spite of its mobility, is on the whole lacking in bright tones, and the *tenebroso* spirit overshadows the whole movement. We might point out a certain similarity in rhythm between the theme of this scherzo and the introductory and main themes from the scherzo of the Fifth Symphony. The two movements also have something in common in the way in which they conclude with a gradual subsidence of sound.

The most significant movement in the quartet is the andante, of which the first theme, a kind of "melodic monologue" reminiscent of oriental music, played by the first violin over a chord accompaniment, is particularly vivid and expressive. Equally expressive is the middle portion of the andante, with a sort of rotating *ostinato* motion in the voices which accompany the theme.

The second theme of the finale recalls the couplets sung by Russian peasants. It is typical of Myaskovsky, however, that no sooner does he introduce this theme and bring out its essentially dance character, then he seems to take fright at its banality and quickly abandons his initial good spirits, shifting the development of the theme into his characteristic nervous and strenuous channels, with sudden storms and lulls, now plunging into the depths of a mysterious gloom (*tutti, con sordini*), now rising to the furious crest of the new and final wave in *tempo prestissimo*.

The C minor quartet, Opus 33, No. 2 (in three movements), preserves the same style as the A minor quartet, but its technique is much simpler. It is also played more often, particularly because of its charming middle movement (andante) with its peculiar nostalgic mood (such as is often heard in broad Russian folk songs) and its poetic, caressing manner, which at times is almost idyllic.

The next quartets—Nos. 5 and 6 (Op. 47, E minor; Op. 49, G minor)—were written in 1939 and 1940, *i.e.*, ten years after the A minor and C minor quartets. By that time Myaskovsky had passed through an extremely important stage in his development, a stage when he was striving to free himself from over-artifice and was seeking simplicity as the highest form of musical expression. The very essence of his music— its content—had also undergone an evolution.

During this period, apart from the 16th Symphony in the heroic style, Myaskovsky composed a number of works in soft lyrical tones, as, for instance, the 15th, 18th and 21st Symphonies, and a fine cycle of romances to words by Lermontov. The Fifth and Sixth Quartets fall within this category. These are Myaskovsky's best essays in the field of chamber music. They are remarkable for their clarity and their variety of mood.

The Fifth Quartet might almost be called a popular piece

for the simplicity of its musical ideas, its emotional content and superb form of expression.

The first movement, written in bright water-color tones, is a lyrical and spontaneous message conveyed in a smooth flow of phrases with rises and falls of a peculiar charm.

The second movement (a brilliant scherzo) opens and closes with a fantastic "rustling" effect with two song episodes in the middle.

The *andantino* (third movement) seems to tell in its principal theme a story of bygone days, rather melancholy and listless. In the middle section of the movement the composer effects, as it were, a return to himself with an *apassionata* theme. The movement closes with a narrative episode.

The highly developed finale, which at times puts us in mind of a romantic symphonized waltz, clashes slightly with the first three movements from the point of view of style, and recalls, rather, Myaskovsky's "middle period," when he wrote the A minor quartet.

The Sixth Quartet (Op. 49, G minor) has the same elements of content and style as the Fifth, but differs from it by virtue of its greater depth of feeling and greater refinement of expression. The marked Russian character of the elegiac themes of the first movement (*moderato*), the captivating melody of the middle theme of the second movement—also in the Russian style (*burlesca, allegro giocoso*)—the melancholy and at times dramatic andante (third movement) and, lastly, the laconic, energetic and virile finale, striking a sharp contrast with all that has gone before—these in general terms are the most impressive qualities of this work.

*   *   *

If one were to choose a quotation to illustrate the creative manner of Myaskovsky in general, and in the vocal genre in particular, one might turn to Baratynsky's *Muse*, which Myaskovsky incidentally set to music among other verses by the same poet (*Meditations*, Op. 1, 1907. Seven poems by E. Baratynsky):

> With blindness by my Muse I am not stricken
> And beautiful she'll ne'er be called, 'tis true.
> No lovesick youths at first sight by her smitten
> Her very shadow ever will pursue.
> She neither has the gift nor inclination
> With play of eyes, or brilliant conversation
> Or delicate adornments to attract.
> 'Tis not so much by her bright, fleeting glance
> As by her speech, serene and simple
> That she astonishes society—
> Which, rather than a stinging condemnation
> Lets fall for her a careless commendation.

It is foreign to the nature of Myaskovsky to strive for external effect. By the very essence of his talent and personal qualities, he is rather the translator of subjective moods evoked from remote depths of thought.

In his first romances (of which he had written about thirty before the First Symphony), Myaskovsky already revealed the dominant tendencies of his vocal style. These early works were characterized by their refined psychology, their subjectivity (often verging on the extreme) and, on the other hand, by a certain pictorial vividness of ideas often met with in the poetry of the Russian symbolists.

Myaskovsky's isolation at that time from democratic trends

both in ideological and political life and in art, the influence
of modernistic fads in literature, his contact with the "Evenings of Modern Music" [2] and, above all, his search for his
own creative individuality—all these served to aggravate his
natural predilection for refined and recherché ideas and
modes of expression. The novel resonances of Balmont's
poetry, the tensely subjective verses of Zinaida Gippius drew
him like a magnet.

Myaskovsky's romances are painted in pessimistic tones.
Their dominant moods are those of weariness, even of hopelessness and isolation from the living world.

Here are a few textual excerpts from romances written during the first period:

> No, not affected; no, not insulted,
> Wearied to death are they, no sparks of life in them.
> I imitate them—I love not anyone,
> I know not anything. I simply sleep.

(Op. 5, No. 3, 1904, *In the Parlor*, words by Zinaida Gippius.)
Or again:

> Your voice no more awakes
> Those sparks sincere.
> Black night within me reigns
> For which no dawn will come!
> The last thin wisp of smoke
> From my dead fire will curl
> And vanish, all too soon
> Unnoticed in the gloom.

---

[2] *Cf.* page 14 (pages 13–14 in this text).

(Op. 21, No. 2, 1922, three sketches to words by Tyut-chev.)

This psychological bent is particularly noticeable in those romances where the real world of sensations is translated into a world of symbols—"Crimson, crimson blood—quiet, quiet heart" (Op. 5, No. 2, 1908, *Blood*, words by Zinaida Gip-pius), or:

> Understand—we're neither here nor there.
> Such is our fate—we are wandering tramps
> And the roosters crow and crow. . . .
> But the heavens still darkly stare.

(Op. 16, No. 6, 1913–1914, *The Cocks*, words by Zinaida Gippius.)

Under the influence of these individualistic moods Myas-kovsky creates an extraordinarily complex world of musical images, a world which is refined to the extreme and at times as if utterly abstract. In some cases, however, he manages to overcome the obscure symbolism of the text by the sheer power of his music and to create convincing works of art in spite of the morbid subtlety of the language. Such, for in-stance, is the music to two poems by Zinaida Gippius: *Un-awares* and *Incantation*. At such moments we feel that, in his approach to and treatment of the texts, Myaskovsky has been influenced by Moussorgsky, especially by *Without the Sun*.

On the other hand the romances to words by Balmont and Ivanov are rather pictorial than psychological, and their musical treatment varies accordingly. In general they tend to be brighter and more optimistic. The melody and harmony are more distinct, while the pictorial resources of the music help the composer to bring out the image which sets the tone of each piece.

For example, in the romance *Temple-Valley*: [3]

> Between the clouds that shroud the hills at eve
> A star peeps out.
> The morning mountain peaks
> Rise from the snows
> All silvered by the moon.
> Along the valley bottom bells are singing,
> Chiming full-tongued.
> Mists are breathing, meadows darken,
> And holy twilight spreads around.
> The spirit of the valley, resonant,
> And silent peaks—
> Are one in worship.

The chief descriptive device here is the chiming of the bells, which is rendered by sustained chords of the ninth and the smooth motion of the accompaniment in triplets. Similar treatment occurs in the romances: *Pan and Psyche* (Ivanov), *The Moon and the Mist* (Zinaida Gippius), *A Full Moon Rose Over the Meadow* (Blok) where the composer paints an evening or nocturnal landscape with its misty lines and endless dream-like calm, the pictorial devices varying in accordance with the nature of the images. At the same time it should be clearly understood that the composer does not attempt to solve any problems of program music.

Myaskovsky's romances are, with but rare exceptions, elegiac or meditative, and there is little variety in the devices employed. In the harmony of their accompaniments the earlier pieces reveal the influences of Rimsky-Korsakov and Debussy.

Myaskovsky's predilection for the two kinds of verse men-

---

[3] Words by Vyacheslav Ivanov.

tioned above (psychological and pictorial) has persisted throughout his career right down to the present day, but the ideological content of his subjects has radically changed. From the extremely subjective and essentially reactionary symbolism of Zinaida Gippius and the impressionistic pictorial effects of Balmont and Ivanov, he has come to the lyrical poetry of Blok and Delvig, and finally to Lermontov and the Soviet poets Shchipachev, Jambul, Lahuti and Kvitko.

The power of expression of Myaskovsky's early romances depends directly on the pianoforte score. The vocal part, which is mainly declamatory, is merely a component of the musical texture as a whole.

But the creation of the Lermontov cycle showed how far Myaskovsky has succeeded in liberating his vocal style from that top-heaviness and over-complication which are so fatal to the spirit of the genre. In most of these later romances the melody is already the decisive element of expression. Furthermore, the element of declamation, while it remains a strong feature of his vocal works, has become melodically rounded off. At the same time the accompaniment has acquired a new simplicity, while retaining its originality and its fidelity to the text.

In his symphonies Myaskovsky traversed a long path, throughout which he preserved all his individuality. So, too, with his romances. The later pieces, in which new content called for new means of expression, bear as plainly as ever the imprint of the composer's personality.

The lyrical element which was, perhaps, best expressed in the music to words by Baratynsky, continued to be the dominant feature in Myaskovsky's later works of the same genre ("Alone I go forth into the road," Op. 40, No. 2; "No, it is not you I love with such ardor," Op. 40, No. 3;

"They loved each other," Op. 40, No. 6; "From an album,"
Op. 40, No. 11).

*   *   *

For the pianoforte Myaskovsky has written a large number
of small pieces (only a part of which has been published)
and several sonatas (four of which have appeared in print).

Much that has been said here about the special features
of Myaskovsky's chamber music and vocal compositions
applies to his works for the pianoforte. Neither in the sonatas
nor in the *bagatelles* is there any external virtuosity, brilliance
or striving for effect.

Myaskovsky's penchant for symphonic treatment betrays
itself in the sonatas no less than in the quartets. The sonatas
reveal, too, the same dynamic quality, logical development
and intense inner pressure as the quartets (Second, Third,
Fourth Sonatas). At the same time there are over-complexi-
ties of expression which are not always justified (as in the
first version of the Third Sonata). The sonatas as a whole
are difficult to play and demand a rather high level of musical
training on the part of the audience.

Myaskovsky's essays in the lighter pianoforte forms are
more simple. Among them, as in the romances, there are
pieces full of lyrical feeling (*cf.* the first and fourth minia-
tures from the cycle of *Whimsies,* the first, second and third
from the cycle *Yellowed Leaves,* etc.), but there are also
pages of music which we can only regard as artificial inven-
tions lacking in emotional appeal.

Although not many of Myaskovsky's works for the piano
have been published, their individuality has gained for them
a place of their own in the history of the Russian pianoforte
style and of the Russian pianoforte sonata in particular.

Musical Technique

In discussing the peculiarities of Myaskovsky's musical idiom there is a tendency among critics of today to regard the "later" Myaskovsky as a "new" Myaskovsky, with respect not only to content but also to style. Thus the critics tend to regard each recent new work of Myaskovsky as a positive *new* phase, employing *new* modes of expression. This somewhat one-sided estimate (consciously or unconsciously, directly or indirectly) throws under a shadow the entire first half of Myaskovsky's symphonic output. This body of the composer's work was once characterized as follows: "Myaskovsky's symphonies do not at once charm the ear or please with that finish, that inertness which is so soothing to the listener—they are explosive, restless." [1] The standpoint of the modern critics seems to be that the merit of Myaskovsky's later works consists above all in their lack of this particular quality and in the appearance of new objective features. Such a conclusion would not be altogether correct. To disregard the superb musical treatment of *Alastor*, the noble imagery of the slow movement of the Second Symphony or the wealth of moods in the Third, or to regard them all merely as expressions of pessimism and "subjectivity" would be tantamount to an underestimation of the composer, a denial of the beginnings of an objectivity which were to

---

[1] Igor Glebov, "Myaskovsky as a Symphonist." *Sovremennaya Muzyka*, April, 1924, p. 74. (Igor Glebov is B. V. Asafyev's pen name.)

develop in his later works. On the other hand, Myaskovsky's
predilection for rather gloomy tones "that do not charm the
ear" is also noticeable in his later works. In short, the composer's stylistic idiosyncrasies should be examined as in a
single context and his "vocabulary" as of a single musical
language. This will obviate the artificial division of Myaskovsky into "old" and "new," "subjective" and "objective."

Myaskovsky's harmony is often said to be "astringent,"
"prickly" and "abrasive." These are first and foremost definitions of personal taste in music, but there is some truth in
them.

Myaskovsky uses an immense diapason of intricate modal-
harmonic formations. This characteristic coupled with others,
equally individual, gives Myaskovsky's music its peculiar
"close-grained" and "dense" quality. If we examine "vertically" a large number of consecutive chords, temporarily
ignoring their interrelations, we shall see how multitonal
they are. We shall see, too, that these chords only rarely occur
in their pure form (irrespective of whether they are formed
by thirds or by fourths). There are nearly always extraneous

Figure 3. Symphony No. 5 (concluding section).

elements in them. Furthermore, the voices are usually crowded closely together, thus contributing to that general effect of "denseness" and congestion to which we have already referred (this applies mainly to the first half of Myaskovsky's work—Figures 3, 4, and 5).

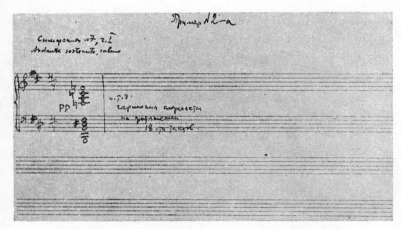

Figure 4. Symphony No. 7, first movement.

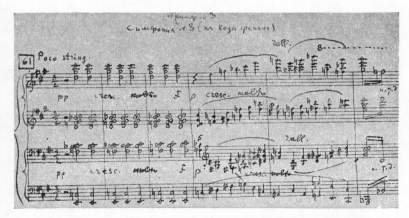

Figure 5. Symphony No. 8 (from the coda of the finale).

The harmonic language is strongly influenced by the linear flow of the part writing. Thanks to the independent movement of the melodies there are some chords which from the point of view of the traditional school of harmony would be defined as accidental combinations. (Figure 6.)

Figure 6. Symphony No. 16, third movement.

The comparatively frequent occurrence of these "accidental harmonic combinations" lends Myaskovsky's music that specific quality which Igor Glebov referred to in the following words: "A striving to connect that which seems unconnectable, to weave together materials which cannot conceivably be woven together, to permeate major with minor, to intensify the tonal functions of chords to extremes of the unexpected—such are the common features of Myaskovsky's works." [2]

Nevertheless it should be pointed out that, from the point

---

[2] *Ibid.*

of view of their harmonic function, the culmination of these constructions, as well as their initial enunciation, is perfectly clear and precise. Thus we are provided with, as it were, "stepping stones," "landmarks" or "pivots," which guide us in following the development of the music, and which are ultimately the foundation of mode or tonality in Myaskovsky. "Tonal relations in Myaskovsky rest on a sure foundation—the consistent interplay of tonic and dominant . . ." [3]

This feature of Myaskovsky's style is observable also in Taneyev, who thought, too, in terms of polyphony—linearity —unlike Glazounov, whose mastery of counterpoint developed within a strict observance of the priority of harmony. With Taneyev, as with Myaskovsky, the harmony is subordinate in general to the movement of the voices, each of which follows its own melodic line.

In some of Myaskovsky's works his linear development or treatment of simultaneous melodies is so free that the tonality or mode is all but obliterated or at any rate seems to be obliterated. Take, for example, the Seventh Symphony, in which there is not a single triad—its modes and functional relations are something apart from the conventional understanding of major and minor; they are explainable only as a result of the composer's polyphonic trend of thought. Other examples may be found in the Tenth and 13th Symphonies.

The character of Myaskovsky's harmonies is also influenced by the peculiar nature of his melodies on the one hand, and, on the other hand, by his methods of developing his musical material. In the first case an immense part is played by the chromatic construction of the themes, which gives rise to a virtually unbroken chain of modulating har-

---

[3] *Ibid.*, p. 72.

monies. This creates a general impression of instability and
harmonic "precariousness" that heightens the tension of the
music. (Figures 7 and 8.)

Figure 7. *Alastor.*

Figure 8. Symphony No. 5, second movement (beginning of *fugato*).

In the second case, sequences, as a typical form of developing the musical material, make it possible both to maintain
the state of tension (thanks to the principle of repetition)
and, depending on the character of the sequences, to weaken
or strengthen it. When the resolution finally supervenes it
usually brings with it new musical material—a new theme.
These are some of the most impressive moments in Myaskovsky's music. The setting-in of such a "calm" after long

tension (instability) creates an unforgettable impression of brightness and clarity.

The development of the first movement of the Fifth Symphony provides examples of this. Each entry of the subordinate theme comes as a kind of "achievement" after arduous "wanderings" (the chromatic treatment in the first theme—Figures 9 and 10).

In other such cases there is an atmosphere of suspense, a feeling of "interruptedness," succeeded by a sense of restored equilibrium and of illumination. Glebov has described this well: "These are rare moments, but they fascinate us with their austere beauty, their sensitiveness and caressing smoothness entirely devoid of crude sensual coloring. Perhaps the most moving examples of such moments occur in *Alastor* and in the Third Symphony. They hold up the movement, yet at the same time impart an aim and a significance to the restlessness around them: the quiet silvery notes of a nocturne seem to penetrate the storm-filled gloom, and in such cases the major tonality usually supervenes and the whole texture of sound becomes transparent and clear, like a fabric flooded with the light of the moon. Only of the moon—not of the sun." [4]

The specific character of Myaskovsky's harmony which makes his thoughts "prickly" and "as hard to grasp as a dog-rose" [5] is also present in his later works. We have only to recall his treatment of the seventh in the slow movements of the 14th and 15th Symphonies, the concluding section of the first movement of the Violin Concerto, the last ten bars of the funeral march in the 16th Symphony (*cf.* Figure 6), the finale of the Fifth Quartet, the introduction of the 21st

---

[4] *Ibid.*, pp. 71–77. [5] *Ibid.*

Symphony and other works, in order to reassure ourselves of
the truth of this.

Thus, in general, Myaskovsky's harmony retains throughout both its linear formation and its "multitonality."

At the same time it must be admitted that these features

Figure 9. Symphony No. 5, first movement (beginning).

Figure 10. Symphony No. 5, first movement (conclusion)

undergo a definite change in accordance with the development of the composer's musical ideas, which he constantly strives to make more expressive by means of an increasing discrimination in his choice of stylistic devices.

For instance, Myaskovsky, with his brilliant mastery of polyphony, uses the fugal form in the finale of the 17th Sym-

Figure 11. Symphony No. 21, introduction.

phony in order to build up a dynamic climax. This remarkable fugue, with its mighty resonances, crowns the entire symphony with its assertion of life triumphant. Similar polyphonic devices in the introduction and conclusion of the 21st Symphony admirably express the unity of thought and mood in the first and last episodes of this work, where the effect of concentration on a single thought (meditation) is achieved to a large extent by constant echoes of the main images of the theme in different voices (Figure 11).

The conclusion of the first movement of the 16th Symphony with its harsh fanfares and unexpected final cadence so vividly underlines the principal idea of the allegro—its impetus and volatility—that a certain over-refinement of the harmonic treatment is justified. We have the same in the funeral march, where the exalted tone of the harmonic accompaniment which appears at its starkest in the climax of the recapitulation (sequences of modified sevenths) is used as a means of emphasizing the funereal and grief-laden character of the music. As for the relatively "simple" harmonies of Myaskovsky's later style, it is a general point to be remembered that it was precisely the new world of ideas which subsequently appeared on the composer's horizon that gave rise to these new and more "simple" harmonies. We put the word simple in quotation marks because we wish to make it quite clear that they did not come of themselves as entirely new expressions fundamentally at odds with Myaskovsky's former style and musical language. They are, indeed, part and parcel of new musical *ideas* whose essence called for different harmonic expression.

In the intermezzo of the 16th Symphony, for example, the *romanza* (first theme) is based harmonically on chords which might be defined as elementary: on a sustained bass there follow the chord of the second, first degree, with diminished sixth; fifth (simple dominant); tonic. The classical precision of the period and the clarity of the functional sequence (tonic-subdominant-dominant-tonic),[6] reduced to an elementary formula with the very first musical statement —these are clear instances of extreme simplicity necessitated by the theme. Something of the same "thinning out" of the harmony was demanded by the themes of the 15th, 17th and 18th Symphonies and the themes of Myaskovsky's last quartets (Fifth and Sixth). In short, the new trends of ideas in

---

[6] And in the second phrase tonic-subdominant-subdominant-tonic.

Myaskovsky and his unending effort to popularize his musical language make for greater simplicity and clarity despite the persistence of all his specific media of musical expression.

*   *   *

The same principle holds true with regard to Myaskovsky's rhythms.

The rhythmic basis of the composer's themes is extremely forceful and impelling. It is this factor, in combination with the ascendant urge of the melodic line, that creates the typical

Figure 12. Symphony No. 6, first movement.

Figure 13. Symphony No. 2, third movement (opening theme).

Figure 14. Symphony No. 3, second movement (opening theme).

dynamic and impetuous quality of his music, particularly in the first and last movements of his symphonies. We need only recall the main themes of the first movements of the Third and Sixth Symphonies or the principal themes from the finals of the Second, Third and other symphonies in order to convince ourselves of this (Figures 12, 13, and 14).

Figure 15. Symphony No. 6, first movement.

For a long period a typical feature of Myaskovsky's music was the use of group rhythms (in various forms) without the recurrence of strong beats inside the bars. The peculiarity of such rhythms considered as forms of expression gives the music an intermittent character and the pulse of the musical phrases becomes disturbed and agitated. The main theme of the first movement of the Third Symphony might serve as an example of this. The Sixth Symphony also begins with this kind of rhythm. It is especially significant where it is intended to express a state of growing tension followed by a "calm." In the Sixth Symphony this applies equally to the develop-

ment of the main theme of the first movement, the passages
leading up to the culmination of the development and the
recapitulation (Figure 15). Equally typical examples of
"spasmodic pulse" and growing tension are to be found in
the Fifth Symphony (the *fugato* from the andante [see
Figure 16]). This same rhythm occurs—and for the same

Figure 16. Symphony No. 5, second movement.

reasons—in the 13th Symphony. There is also the same origin
to some highly characteristic rhythmic formations which
Myaskovsky repeatedly uses in the slow movements of his
symphonies, in musical episodes of a rather specific nature
from the point of view of their psychological design.

This rhythm is created by syncopation, pauses or the tying
of strong beats, and the utilization of relatively insistent
sounds, "white notes" (Figures 17 and 18 [7]). In such

---

[7] From the transitional section of the first movement—Ninth Symphony.
This material is also included in the third movement—andante.

episodes, which are devoid of any definite descriptive purpose, the music conveys with extraordinary power a general impression of concentrated meditation.

Figure 17. Symphony No. 15, second movement.

Figure 18. Symphony No. 9, first movement.

Generally speaking Myaskovsky's rhythms are intricate and extremely changeable. But he has favorite groups of rhythms which, though not identical, have something in common if they are analyzed deeply enough. Apart from the examples referred to above, we might point out his use of rhythmic groups made up of short, broken phrases of four,

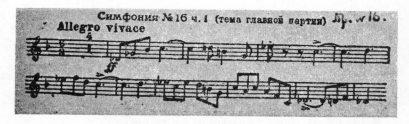

Figure 19. Symphony No. 16, first movement (main theme).

Figure 20. Symphony No. 21 (main theme).

five or more beats, as for instance in the first theme of the third movement of the Second Symphony (Figure 13). There are similar instances in the first theme of the second movement of the Third Symphony (Figure 14); and to a lesser degree in the first theme of the finale of the Fourth Symphony; the first themes of the first movement (Figure 12), and scherzo of the Sixth Symphony; the *fugato* of the second movement of the Seventh Symphony, and the second theme of the introduction to the third movement of the 11th Symphony.

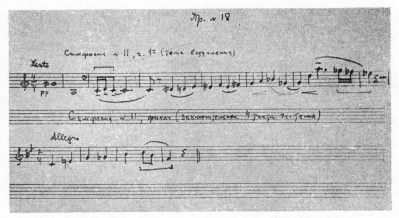

Figure 21. Symphony No. 11, first movement (opening theme) and finale (including four bars of the principal theme).

The same basic rhythmic characteristics operate throughout the whole of Myaskovsky's musical output. Both his themes from the 14th to the 21st Symphonies and those of his earlier compositions are saturated with mobile and sharp rhythms. But this does not mean that there is no change, no development in his work in this respect. The spasmodic, agitated rhythms without strong beats tend to be replaced by rhythms based on strong beats. Thus the more recent works of Myaskovsky, while preserving the mobile, dynamic qualities of his earlier works, become more even, tranquil and finished (Figures 19 and 20).

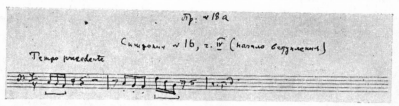

Figure 22. Symphony No. 16, fourth movement (opening bars of the introduction).

Figure 23. Symphony No. 15, fourth movement (opening theme of the introduction).

There are, moreover, several favorite patterns of rhythm, one of which recurs particularly often after the Tenth Symphony. It consists of two equally short beats followed by a long beat, or of three consecutive short beats.

As instances of this we may cite the theme of the introduction to the first movement and the theme of the finale of the 11th Symphony (Figure 21), the theme of the introduction to the fourth movement of the 16th Symphony

Figure 23a. Symphony No. 20, first movement (principal theme).

(Figure 22), the theme of the introduction to the fourth movement of the 15th Symphony (Figure 23), the principal theme of the first movement of the 17th Symphony and the principal theme of the first movement of the 20th Symphony (Figure 23a).

These rhythmic groups and elements create an atmosphere of assurance and purpose in contrast to the troubled effect of some of the patterns referred to above.

*   *   *

As regards what is perhaps the most important means of musical expression—melody—it may safely be said that it is here, above all, that a clear evolution in Myaskovsky's musical idiom can be traced. Two general types of melody stand out in his work. To the first of these belong his melodies conceived in the folk idiom.

Here we find the rather extensive use of melodic phrases in the *berceuse* manner: for instance the *Lullaby* to words by Balmont; the cradle song in the andante of the Fifth Symphony (used by Myaskovsky as a symbol of night); the

Figure 24. Symphony No. 5, second movement.

cradle-song elements in the andante and allegro of the Sixth Symphony; the cradle song in the second movement of the Seventh Symphony (first theme); the cradle-song idiom in the song about the soldier's wife in the Eighth Symphony, and the music (romance) to Lermontov's *Cossack Lullaby*.

To this same type also belong the broad melodies reminiscent of the traditional long-drawn-out Russian folk songs: for instance, the subordinate theme of the first movement of the Fifth Symphony; the spiritual in the finale of the Sixth Symphony (expressing the parting of the soul from the body); the theme of the song about the soldier's wife in the andante (third movement) of the Eighth Symphony mentioned above; some themes from the orchestral suites, Opus 32; the theme (clarinet) of the introduction to the 12th Symphony; the opening theme in the andante of the 15th Symphony; the subordinate theme of the first movement of the 16th Symphony; one of the themes from the andante of the 18th Symphony; one of the themes from the andante of the Fifth Symphony (Figure 24), etc.

Of different character, but nevertheless coming within the same category, are Myaskovsky's dance themes. These

Figure 25. Symphony No. 14, second movement.

melodies have fairly consistent peculiarities—they are diatonic (with rare chromatic passages), clear in outline (with sharply defined phrases and periods), lilting, broad, and flowing. In other words, they have all the elements of his themes in the folk idiom (Figure 25).

Myaskovsky imparts his own peculiar prickliness and tartness to these themes by certain chromatic changes of intonation both in the melody (especially on the second, fourth and seventh) and in the corresponding harmonies. But this deliberate "artificiality" is only a stylistic device which never severs the threads binding the melody to its prime source—folk music.

This brings us to the second category of Myaskovsky's musical images.

In the first category the melodies have a common diatonic quality. In the second they are typified by their chromatic nature. In the first category the melodies are broad, pure and songlike. In the second we find broken lines, "short breathing," and progressions which are essentially orchestral and could scarcely be rendered by the human voice. The actual *motifs* on which the melodic pattern is based are abrupt.

In the first category the rhythms are varied and rich but smooth, while in the second they are sharp, impulsive, sometimes confident, but more often nervously exalted. These latter rhythms abound in Myaskovsky's music but are perhaps best exemplified in the theme of the *Alastor,* the first theme of the third movement (finale) of the Second Symphony, and virtually all the themes of the Third and Fourth Symphonies. In this connection we might also recall the *fugato* in the second movement of the Seventh Symphony (referred to above, p. 96), the opening themes of the first and second movements (allegro and scherzo) of the Sixth Symphony, and a number of themes from the quartets, sonatas and other compositions.

We have noted that the evolution of Myaskovsky is most clearly traced in his melodies. Here we should bear in mind, above all, the folk-song idiom which covers a wide range in the second phase of his work. The folk element, in fact, makes itself felt with increasing emphasis in his later works, where it bears fruit in a wealth of lovely melodies.

Moreover, those of the more recent melodies which are Myaskovsky's own individual creation reveal certain positive traits that tend to become increasingly stabilized. They are more sustained and more highly developed than those of the earlier works, and have greater force. And yet, from the point of view of formal length, they are not so different from Myaskovsky's earlier melodies. The main tendency seems to consist in a gradual elimination of the "broken-off" effect and tonal confusion of the earlier melodies, as a result of which they often seemed spasmodic, unfinished and fragmentary.

This increasing vocalization of Myaskovsky's melodies brings them nearer to the living breath of real life and toward a more direct expression of mood and feeling. The entire 17th Symphony is permeated with such melodies; they are numerous in the 16th, 20th and 21st Symphonies, and in the later quartets.

*   *   *

The prime tool of a symphonist is the orchestra, and his prime medium is instrumentation. Outwardly Myaskovsky would seem to stand nearest of all to the Glazounov school in his use of the orchestra. But such a comparison would give a far from adequate idea of Myaskovsky's orchestration. For all their density of texture Glazounov's orchestrations are highly colorful, intensely descriptive, and filled with light, although this light might rather be compared with the red hues of a sunset than with the fires of early morning. Myaskovsky's orchestration lacks this luminosity. It reminds us of a score by Brahms which moved a certain conductor to say "The sun never shines in it." [8] Myaskovsky is no colorist. In his handling of the orchestra he is an artist only of "black and white, in whom the darker tones predominate—dense, gloomy, and lowering." [9]

---

[8] Quoted from Adam Carse, *A History of Orchestration*, p. 229.
[9] Igor Glebov, "Myaskovsky as a Symphonist." *Sovremennaya Muzyka*, April, 1924; p. 72.

This criticism, which holds true of a certain phase of Myaskovsky's work, no longer applies to his musical output as a whole. We have only to glance at the scores of Symphonies 14 to 21 and at the Violin Concerto to see that Glebov's characterization is now wide of the mark, especially its latter half.

One of the most striking developments that can be traced in Myaskovsky's work is the growing richness of his orchestral palette and, above all, an added brightness. It need scarcely be pointed out that this gradual "effulgence" of the composer's style has gone hand in hand with corresponding changes in his ideas and in his general artistic outlook.

Thus, in the course of his evolution, Myaskovsky has found ways and means of brightening the orchestral tone color of his symphonies. We become conscious of a deliberate tendency to accentuate the melodic line, to "lift it" above the accompaniment, to find stronger contrasts in the treatment of various episodes. No less significant is the tendency to increase the range of the parts. An example of this is the instrumentation of the second themes in the first movements of the Fifth and 16th Symphonies. These two themes have much in common, and it is not surprising to find them assigned to the same instruments (first and second clarinets, bassoons, first and second violas and 'cellos) in the same registers and with the same treatment of voices (*divisi*). But they sound differently. The cramped spacing of the parts and the doubling of the voices throughout in the Fifth Symphony create an effect of greater fullness and density. The comparatively wide spacing of the parts and the remote pitch of the bass in the 16th Symphony, however, create an atmosphere of spaciousness and "airiness" and, other conditions being equal, lend the music a lighter and brighter color. The further development of both themes serves only to corroborate this point of view. The second entry of the theme in the Fifth Symphony (wood and brass) intensifies the initial coloring, while the sonority of the low registers of the woodwind and brass adds a touch of gloomy solemnity. In the 16th Symphony, the development of the music leads to a diametrically opposite effect. The second entry of the themes in the high registers of the flute and oboe—where their timbre is brightest (thus emphasizing the melodic line and increasing the diapason of sound)—in conjunction with the change of rhythm in the bass—from the sustained minims in the first statement to the measured anapaestic pulsation of the second (♩ ♫ ♩ ♫ ♩)— naturally brings out and intensifies the bright features of the music, making it more vocal and flexible, and giving it an optimistic ring.

A comparison of corresponding movements in the Third and 16th Symphonies (the coda of the second movement of the Third Symphony—*marche funèbre*—and the funeral march from the third movement of the 16th Symphony) reveals similar differences of orchestral treatment. In the first place the orchestral coloring of the 16th Symphony differs from that of the Third in the treatment of the introduction to the march. In the Third Symphony there is no contrast in the orchestration between the introduction to the march and the march proper. The low registers of the strings predominate throughout. The analogous introductory recitative in unison in the 16th Symphony, however, is given to the brass alone (trombones and tubas), while the entry of the march theme itself is taken by the strings. This creates a considerable contrast in color. The theme of the march as played by the strings seems brighter and softer as compared with the introduction, while at the same time none of the essential austerity and virility of the music is lost. Furthermore, in the orchestration of the later march, we are conscious of an unmistakable effort on the part of the composer to bring the melodic line into higher relief and to make the harmonic background more transparent, more economical and less obtrusive.

Thus one of the most important features of the evolution of Myaskovsky's orchestral technique, an evolution which forms an integral part of the composer's general growth to maturity as a whole, is his increasing striving after higher relief and "sculptural" effects.

*   *   *

No study of Myaskovsky's style would be complete without a brief consideration of certain peculiarities of form in his symphonies.

In the first place attention should be drawn to the construction of his first movements—sonata allegros. The expositions reveal a choice of thematic material and a manner of developing it that produce the most striking contrasts, while at the same time the contrasted ideas remain integrally related and complementary to each other. The themes are set forth in the exposition with such masterly laconicism and force that recourse to the normal transitional and episodic passages becomes superfluous. For instance, in the exposition of the 16th Symphony, the subordinate theme follows *immediately* on the tail of the main theme; between these two subjects Myaskovsky introduces no other thematic material. The first subject flows straight into the second through the repetition of the principal rhythmic groups of the main theme. These rhythmic groups perform the function of a transition. We find Beethoven treating his expositions in the same way, for instance, in the Fifth Symphony.

Another method whereby Myaskovsky "hides the seams" and attains unity of statement in his sonata allegros is connecting the first and second subjects with thematic material of such significance and coherence that it acquires a status of its own and ceases to be subordinate. In such cases the music of the exposition flows in a single stream unbroken by the transitional passages which it contains. For example, in the 17th Symphony between the main and subordinate themes of the exposition there is a broadly developed transition consisting of two fine images which, in both mood and technical construction, are akin to the principal subjects of the exposition. The rhythmic group ♩ ♫ ♩ of these images connects them with the first theme of the exposition, while their melodic line leads directly to, and merges with the second. (This treatment is also characteristic of other compositions—the Fourth Symphony, first movement; the Sixth Symphony, first movement, etc.) At the same time the general emotional content of the transition serves to soften the exultation of the first theme by adding a note of rapturous dreaminess.

In his development and treatment of his thematic material Myaskovsky relies mainly on the devices of polyphony— imitation, canon, *fugato*, augmentation, diminution, superimposition. It may be confidently asserted that as a master of this technique Myaskovsky is outstanding among contemporary composers. It was precisely this predilection for polyphonic treatment, however, that was criticized by Glebov: "We personally are daunted only by the author's weakness for canon and imitation. The composer has so full and free a mastery of the genuine contrapuntal style that he could afford to employ less frequently devices which, for all their masterliness, are somewhat superficial. He could afford to resort less frequently to artificialities of counterpoint which, when they are repeated too often, tend to blunt the sincerity of his music and threaten to degenerate into a besetting habit." [10]

The general effect of Myaskovsky's themes is driven home with full force in his culminations. These culminations are, as a rule, created from material which is new in relation to all that has gone before it, and the composer's way of preparing for them with the introduction of the new images on which they are built is one of the most impressive aspects of his manner. As examples of this, which are extremely numerous, we need only refer to the first movements of the First, Third, Fifth, Sixth, 14th, 16th and other symphonies.

Myaskovsky's recapitulations generally repeat his expositions without important changes. Their lack of new impetus, however, does not lead to any slackening off in the general tension of the music. On the other hand, coming as it does after a powerful culmination, when the elaboration of the material has been carried to a climax, the entry of the recapitulation is accepted as a new stage in the development of the movement as a whole.

Myaskovsky achieves this same sense of novelty in the coda. In some cases he grafts on to the coda what promises to be a second development of the exposition and builds up a new culmination, thereby invoking a sense of the impending development in the following movement (cf. the 11th, 15th and 17th Symphonies and the Violin Concerto). Or again he relaxes the tension in the coda and for a short spell (short in comparison to what has gone before) contrasts the tranquillity of the close with the storm and stress of the exposition, development and recapitulation. (Superb examples of this are the first movements of the Fifth, Sixth and 14th Symphonies.)

[10] Igor Glebov on Myaskovsky's *Alastor*. *Muzyka*, No. 198, 1914.

It may be stated, in conclusion, that Myaskovsky's sonata allegro derives on the one hand from Beethoven and on the other hand from Tchaikovsky.

In the middle sections of his works Myaskovsky has a preference for slow rather than quick movements. While his music may be dynamic and impelling as a general rule, it is often contemplative and imbued with a meditative lyricism. Thus he not only prefers slow movements in his middle sections but occasionally even removes the scherzo altogether from the scheme of things and leaves his symphonies with three parts. Thus the First, Second, Fourth, 11th, 18th, and 20th Symphonies are three-movement pieces with slow movements in the middle.

If the first movements of Myaskovsky's symphonies are highly explosive and dramatic, these middle movements on the other hand are intensely contemplative and lyrical, and the composer's andantes and adagios reveal a brightness of coloring, a profoundly lyrical and thoughtful content and a nobility of expression that seem to belie his general predilection for disturbed and "sunless" tones. The slow movements of the First, Fourth, Ninth, 11th, 17th and 20th Symphonies constitute some of the best pages in his music.

Moreover, while differing in construction from Myaskovsky's sonata allegros, his slow movements seem to grow naturally out of them. Myaskovsky's symphonies, indeed, are built not only on the general principle of contrast (allegro-andante) but also with a view to the underlying, organic unity of development of each work taken as a whole. He frequently constructs his andantes on thematic material closely related to or having at least certain traits in common with what has gone before. For instance, in the Sixth Symphony both the theme of the introduction to the third movement and the pastoral episode form links with the scherzo. In the andante of the Ninth Symphony Myaskovsky uses thematic material taken both from the transitional section of the first movement and from the scherzo. In other cases the main theme of the andante, in contrast with its transitional first and last passages, recalls the mood of the sonata allegro, although it does not actually repeat the musical content of the first movement. A vivid example of this treatment is the Fifth Symphony, where the powerful growth of tension in the *fugato* of the andante re-echoes the development of the allegro and leads to a similar culmination of sound and dramatic effect.

For the most part Myaskovsky brings out the character of the scherzo by using elements of popular music or song and dance themes, as, for example, in the Fifth, Eighth, 17th and, to a lesser degree, in the 14th Symphony. In the 15th and 19th Symphonies Myaskovsky has recourse to the waltz genre. As a general rule he uses the scherzo, which stands out in sharp contrast with the deeply contemplative mood of the slow movement, in order to impart an added realism to his symphonies, bringing them "closer to earth."

The finales vary according to the general conception and design of the work as a whole.[11] In the Third Symphony the function of a finale is performed by a coda based on the theme of the funeral march. The brighter finales of the Fourth and Fifth Symphonies are the result of less personal moods and reflect to a greater extent the composer's consciousness of objective reality. In the Sixth Symphony, as we pointed out elsewhere, the finale is a summation of the fundamental idea which runs through the entire work: the conflict between life and death. Of course, not all the concluding sections of

---

[11] Myaskovsky's favorite form in the finale is the rondo.

Myaskovsky's symphonies are equally convincing. Insufficient conciseness in the development of musical ideas detracts from the finales of the 19th Symphony, the Violin Concerto, and, to some extent, also of the 14th Symphony. On the whole, it may be stated, however, that despite all the complexity of this genre, the symphonies of Myaskovsky are highly convincing in the development of their dramatic content. They are integral, coherent productions, united by a single, comprehensive idea.

In conclusion I should like to quote one of Igor Glebov's fine observations on Myaskovsky as a symphonist:

". . . But perhaps his most important trait is his unswerving fidelity to the principles of the sonata allegro. . . . Myaskovsky has not passed by any of the significant trends in contemporary music without duly evaluating it and weighing it in the balance. His individual cast of thought attracts him to large cyclic forms and intricate compositions. His predominantly intellectual approach, as his main guiding influence, obliges him to submit to an extraordinarily severe, iron-rigid discipline of part writing. Having convinced himself of the vitality, flexibility and logic of the essential principles of musical construction as evolved by European culture, Myaskovsky, with an astonishing power of thought, amid the debris of obsolete schemes, devices, traditions and rules, amid the decrepitude of outworn static forms, raises the banner of the ceaseless quest for new avenues in modern life and finds a rational, stable and vital organizing principle in the symphonic form as the product of a long process of *natural selection*, a phenomenon still pregnant with possibilities and an organism capable of further development. . . ." [12]

---

[12] Igor Glebov, "Myaskovsky as a Symphonist." *Sovremennaya Muzyka*, April, 1924; pp. 72–73.

Conclusion

Myaskovsky is often spoken of as a "thinker" and "philosopher." These definitions correctly stress the profundity of his music. The theme of Man tempted by the Demon in the tone poem *The Vow of Silence,* the theme of the romantic hero Alastor, whose death is an act of proud self-abnegation, the themes of Revolution and once more of death in the Sixth Symphony, of Stepan Razin in the Eighth, of Eugene from Pushkin's *Bronze Horseman* in the Tenth and of the collectivization of the countryside in the 12th—all these subjects, together with the great lyric and heroic themes of the composer's later works, possess, notwithstanding their essential diversity, the same universality of thought and philosophic content.

By virtue of the depth of his ideas, the emotional content of his music and his mode of thinking, Myaskovsky continues and develops the symphonic principles of Tchaikovsky on the one hand, while on the other hand he reveals certain of the peculiarities of the symphonic style of Taneyev and Glazounov.

A search for the roots of Myaskovsky's style, however, takes us beyond the bounds of Russian music. In the last analysis his work represents a development of the principles upon which Beethoven's symphonies rest. Myaskovsky's depth of ideas, his dynamic quality, his austerity—at times approaching asceticism—and his unswerving loyalty to the principles of the sonata allegro place his compositions in a class with those of the great classic composer.

After the 19th century the history of the Russian symphony is associated primarily with the names of Glazounov, Taneyev, Scriabin and Myaskovsky, for the brilliant works of Rachmaninov, Lyadov, Stravinsky, Prokofieff and other of Myaskovsky's contemporaries cannot be considered as landmarks in the development of the symphonic genre in Russian musical culture.[1]

Myaskovsky thus carries on the line of Russian symphonic music: he is, as it were, a connecting link between the old and new eras. The tragic confusion that prevailed in the mind of the Russian intelligentsia during the pre-revolutionary years, the peculiar "self-denying" yet profoundly sincere acceptance of the Revolution characteristic of certain prominent representatives of the world of art in those early days, the gradual assimilation of new ideas and emotions under the influence of the Soviet environment—all found their expression in his music.

Myaskovsky is an extremely prolific composer. Only in the 18th century, when purely instrumental music flourished to an unprecedented degree, do we find composers who produced such a vast quantity of music in the symphonic genre. The volume of Myaskovsky's work speaks eloquently of his mastery of the complex technique of symphonic composition.

The importance of technical skill as the *sine qua non* of

---

[1] The rôle of the younger generation of composers—Shostakovich, Shebalin, Kabalevsky, Khachaturyan, and others—in the development of Soviet instrumental, and especially symphonic music, lies beyond the scope of the present work. The allied questions of the influence of the older generation of composers on the younger and of what has been accomplished by Soviet composers in general in the domain of the symphony are likewise subjects which call for separate treatment.

all art was deeply appreciated by the great Russian musicians of the past. When he wrote his first opera, *Daughter of Pskov*, Rimsky-Korsakov, for instance, was greatly handicapped by his inability to express his ideas exactly as he would have wished and keenly felt his own shortcomings in this respect: ". . . My lack of harmonic and contrapuntal technique, shortly after the completion of *Daughter of Pskov*, prevented me from giving full rein to my imagination which began to revert again and again to the old hackneyed devices. It was only by developing this technique that I was able to break fresh ground and to infuse new life into my work." [2]

Tchaikovsky, too, repeatedly stressed the need for systematic effort. "Sometimes inspiration eludes one," he said. "But I consider it the *bounden duty* of an artist never to succumb, for *laziness* is very strong in all of us. One must never wait for inspiration. She does not willingly visit the lazy; she comes only to those who summon her." [3]

Of Myaskovsky, as of these great Russian composers, it may be truly said that inspiration and labor were his lifelong companions.

When we speak of Myaskovsky as a symphonist, we must not forget his chamber music. Notwithstanding the essential differences in treatment between the symphony and the sonata or quartet, the principles of Myaskovsky's symphony writing apply in large measure also to his chamber music. His pianoforte sonatas and quartets, indeed, by the nature of their thematic material and development, have been defined by Glebov as miniature symphonies.

It was natural that Myaskovsky's chamber music, which

---

[2] Rimsky-Korsakov, *Chronicle of My Musical Life*, Chapter X, p. 133.
[3] Correspondence with Mme. von Meck, Vol. I, Letter No. 163, p. 372.

was written simultaneously with his symphonies, should bear the same traits and the same general content as his larger works. Hence the evolution of his symphonic style covers in essence the evolution of his style in chamber music. It should not be forgotten, however, that Myaskovsky used his pianoforte works, and especially the romances of the first period of his career as a composer, for experimenting in problems of style. The smaller works can in a sense be considered as sketches for larger compositions, and from this standpoint they are of particular interest to the student of Myaskovsky, inasmuch as they are of great help in enabling us to trace the development of his style.

Myaskovsky's chamber music is, of course, of less importance than his symphonic works. Nevertheless, some of his compositions in this genre are of considerable merit and occupy a place of honor in the history of chamber music as a whole. To this category belong first of all his quartets, particularly the Fourth, Fifth and Sixth, which are distinguished for their depth of ideas, plasticity of form and beauty of tone color; the lovely pianoforte sonata in F-sharp minor which is highly characteristic of the early rebellious period in the composer's career; and a number of songs, especially the vocal cycles to poems by Lermontov, Baratynsky and Balmont.

One of the most remarkable features of Myaskovsky's music is its originality. Even the folk *motifs* he uses bear the strong imprint of his personality, without, however, losing anything of their specific nature. Such *motifs* in Myaskovsky's music are usually his own discoveries. Quotations or "rehashes" are extremely rare.

Myaskovsky's music compared, let us say, to Tchaikovsky's is farther from "that extensive field of musical idioms that belong to everyday life and the sum of which, at a given historical moment, occupies a place of considerable importance and stability in the artistic culture of a country." [4] Tchaikovsky is not afraid of "commonplace or trivial intonations," so long as they remain "true and accurate vehicles of the emotion he seeks to convey." [5]

In Myaskovsky's music there are fewer familiar tunes or phrases. Hearing his works for the first time we are struck rather by their highly individual treatment.

Tchaikovsky's music is replete with familiar, everyday intonations. It is true that his music is also extremely original, and can be immediately recognized by two or three melodic phrases. But Myaskovsky's originality is of a specific nature. It is contained chiefly in a certain "difference" and exclusiveness of his music. And, if on the one hand, this renders it more difficult to grasp and appreciate, on the other hand it contributes to that organic unity and polish of style that make Myaskovsky so important a phenomenon in Russian music today.

Myaskovsky's originality is devoid of all eccentricity and pseudo-estheticism. To use an expression of Sergei Prokofieff's, he never "exchanges winks with the public."

By all this we do not mean to imply that Myaskovsky has not been subjected to certain influences. It is interesting to note the composer's own understanding of the word "influence." Myaskovsky considers that to employ a method, modulation or scheme used by some other composer means to be influenced by him. In this sense his music, on his own admission, bears the influence of Scriabin and Glazounov. His

---

[4] Igor Glebov, *In Memory of Peter Ilyich Tchaikovsky*, 1940, p. 19.
[5] *Ibid.*

Second and Third Symphonies are close to Scriabin. The latter again appears in Myaskovsky's First Symphony, the development of which begins in precisely the same manner as Scriabin's Third. "On the whole," says Myaskovsky, "I am a follower of Tchaikovsky, Metner, Rachmaninov and, above all, of the 'Big Five.' [6] . . . By this I mean to say that I class myself with them [Rimsky-Korsakov, Glazounov, Lyadov and their schools]. Although, of course, it would be difficult to say exactly where to look for Rimsky-Korsakov in my symphonies, for example. In such a case perhaps it would be more exact to refer to Glazounov." [7]

Actually, however, the influence of the Russian classics can be found in the general spirit and character of Myaskovsky's music rather than in any direct, concrete reflection. For Myaskovsky is a truly Russian composer. In this respect he is akin not only to Scriabin and Glazounov but also to Moussorgsky, Tchaikovsky and Rimsky-Korsakov.

In this connection it is worthy of note that, in the initial stages of his career when ideas of tragic despair dominated his work, Myaskovsky was very near in his use of tone color to Moussorgsky, particularly to the Moussorgsky of the later (*Without the Sun*) period. Subsequently, *i.e.,* after his 12th and 13th Symphonies Myaskovsky sometimes comes surprisingly and unexpectedly close to the radiant, warm images of Rimsky-Korsakov (*cf.* the themes of Volkhova from *Sadko* and Martha from *The Tsar's Bride*). It is significant, too, that, with the possible exception of a few passages in the Eighth and to an even lesser extent in the 11th Symphony, there is very little of Borodin in Myaskovsky's music. Myas-

---

[6] *Cf.* footnote 8 on page 9.
[7] From a conversation with Myaskovsky—A. I.

kovsky was indeed far from the calm epic world of Borodin. His natural dramatic and lyric bent brought him closer to Tchaikovsky, Moussorgsky and Rimsky-Korsakov.

Of all Myaskovsky's numerous activities, least of all has been said about his work as a critic, to which he devoted three and a half years (from 1911 to 1914) as reviewer for the weekly *Muzyka*. The traits so characteristic of him—clarity and precision in passing judgment, thorough knowledge of his subject, and strict adherence to principle—manifested themselves even in this early period of his independent professional career.

In one of his articles Myaskovsky elaborates the principles he considers to be basic in the appraisal of any piece of music.

"The first thing I demand from music in general is *directness of appeal, power and nobility* of expression; music that does not satisfy these three requirements does not exist for me, or if it does exist, then it does so solely for utilitarian purposes.

". . . I always consider a piece of music from three points of view: its content, its inner and its outer form. . . .

"Of the three elements enumerated above I consider the first two to be absolutely essential: I admire good outer form, but I can make allowances for imperfections in it provided that the first two elements are beyond reproach." [8] (Incidentally, nowadays Myaskovsky does not make any such allowances.)

Judging classic and contemporary music by these standards Myaskovsky has given a positive appraisal of the works

---

[8] "N. Metner—Impressions of His Personality as an Artist." *Muzyka*, No. 119, 1913, pp. 150–152.

of Debussy, Stravinsky (*Petrouchka, Sacre du Printemps, Firebird,* First Symphony), Metner and others.

While admiring the composers of the Russian school—Rimsky-Korsakov, Borodin and Moussorgsky—for their wealth of content, Myaskovsky was critical of Glazounov for the latter's emphasis on pure form.

". . . I place Moussorgsky on an equal footing with Tchaikovsky and Scriabin, and reject Glazounov and his whole school, although I myself, unfortunately, am still enmeshed in its nets. . . . His external form is magnificent, but the *inner structure* [italics mine—A. I.] of his music does not always stand close scrutiny, especially in his longer works. . . ." [9]

In the sphere of symphonic music Myaskovsky was the first critic to speak of Tchaikovsky as having continued the symphonic line laid down by Beethoven, thereby not only defending the work of the great Russian composer from unjust attacks on the part of certain St. Petersburg musical circles at the time, but also placing him in the same class with Beethoven.

Myaskovsky was likewise one of the first musical critics to appreciate the talents of Stravinsky and Sergei Prokofieff.

As a publicist [10] Myaskovsky was an ardent champion of Russian art, and advocated the popularization of Russian artists, professionals and newcomers alike, by incorporating their works in the programs of public concerts. A striking example of the pointedness of his literary style and of his high-

---

[9] By "inner structure" Myaskovsky means the development and interchange of moods and emotions.

[10] In three and a half years the composer wrote sixty miscellaneous articles and reviews. It should be noted that all this work was done by Myaskovsky without remuneration.

principled judgment is the article in *Muzyka*, 1914, attacking
A. Ziloti, the famous conductor, for his partiality toward foreign composers (and not always the best!) while ignoring so
gifted a Russian musician as Sergei Prokofieff.[11]

A complete and exhaustive analysis of the work and activities of Myaskovsky has yet to be made. Many of his works
are still insufficiently known. A large number of his early
compositions, which are of great interest in tracing the development of his style, as well as a number of later symphonic
works (*e.g.*, *Petite Ouverture*, 1909; *Sinfonietta*, 1910; *Preludio e fughetta* on the name of "Saradgef" [Sarajev], 1934;
the 13th and 17th Symphonies), are still in manuscript.

Moreover, many of Myaskovsky's large and small works
(chamber pieces, especially songs), although published, are
virtually unknown to the public for the reason that they are
rarely performed and difficult to acquire. Such works as the
tone poem *The Vow of Silence*, the Second, Seventh, Eighth,
Tenth, 11th, 13th and—of his later works—the 15th and 17th
Symphonies, have been performed only once or twice, or at
best three times. It is not surprising, therefore, that there are
so few detailed studies of his work of a type calculated to meet
the present demand.[12]

Another reason why Myaskovsky is still insufficiently
known is that there have been up to date all too few really
intelligent performances of his works capable of giving an
adequate picture of the composer's ideas, emotions and technical mastery. Before Beethoven won recognition as a symphonist he had to interpret his own works; later on, his symphonies were performed under the direction of Berlioz,

---

[11] *Muzyka*, No. 178, 1914, pp. 334–336.
[12] The splendid articles on Myaskovsky by Igor Glebov unfortunately do
not include the composer's later compositions.

Weber, Wagner, von Bülow and other outstanding conductors. Tchaikovsky had such inspired interpreters as Nikolai Rubinstein and Arthur Nikisch, followed by the leading conductors of every country in the world, to expound and popularize his music. But the dramatic quality and the conflicting elements in Myaskovsky's music—his pessimism on the one hand and his vitality on the other—have not yet found a worthy interpreter (the isolated successful performances by Sarajev, Golovanov, Ivanov and others are unfortunately too few as compared with the volume of Myaskovsky's work).

The music, life and activity of Myaskovsky are an integral part of Soviet culture as a whole. With his artist's intuition, the composer expressed in the early period of his work (coincident with the interim between the 1905 and 1917 Revolutions) the mood of that section of the Russian intelligentsia which, sensing the inevitability of the approaching storm, was in a state of mental confusion, spiritual depression and vague rebellion (*Alastor, The Vow of Silence,* the Second and Third Symphonies, several of the romances, etc.).

The Great Socialist October Revolution cleared the oppressive atmosphere of this pre-revolutionary period. Those who accepted it, even if they did not fully grasp what had happened, were drawn into its orbit and sooner or later "found themselves" and took their places as builders of the new life.

Myaskovsky's Sixth Symphony (1922–1923) is a striking artistic document, revealing how deeply the Revolution affected him. True, he saw it through the prism of his own "intellectual, neurasthenic perceptions," as he himself puts it. But the tragic hopelessness of the Third Symphony and the apotheosis of death in *Alastor* are no longer present.

At the present time Myaskovsky is seeking tirelessly to

produce music that would give a faithful reflection of Soviet reality. His interest in Soviet subject matter, and the use of folk melodies, song and dance *motifs* and lyrical images characteristic of his later works are indicative of his persistent quest for a realistic musical language. Even after the vivid 15th Symphony he wrote: "Nevertheless this is not yet the idiom I seek in order to feel that I am truly an artist of my day." [13]

The 21st Symphony is one of Myaskovsky's best; it constitutes a link in a long chain of search for perfection. A work of outstanding artistic merit, which has won wide recognition, this symphony is a fitting expression of the enrichment of the inner world of the artist that became possible only under the conditions of Socialism.

One of Myaskovsky's most fundamental traits, indeed, is his deep consciousness of the great tasks facing Soviet art in general. "My lifelong ambition," he writes, "of expressing in music feelings associated with the personalities of our great contemporaries, who are building up society anew with such remarkable foresight, courage and wisdom, is constantly frustrated by the obvious immaturity of my technique. . . . Nevertheless, such is still my dream and I feel sure that one day it will come true, just as the most cherished dreams of the best representatives of humanity during the past ages have come true with us." [14]

---

[13] "Autobiographical Notes."
[14] *Ibid.*

Myaskovsky's Music During the Great Patriotic War

Soviet artists have produced many outstanding works since the outbreak of the war. Art in all its diverse forms has taken its place as an indispensable spiritual weapon for both front and rear. The remarkable thing is that it has not become purely utilitarian in the process. On the contrary, wartime art is notable both for its wealth of ideas and beauty of form. In this respect Soviet composers occupy a leading position. The work of Prokofieff, Shostakovich, Myaskovsky, Zakharov, Khachaturyan and many other masters of Russian music has won widespread recognition both in the Soviet Union and abroad.

When the war broke out Nikolai Myaskovsky, one of the leading symphonic writers of our day and representative of the older generation of composers, was in his sixties with a long and fruitful life of creative effort behind him. Nevertheless he responded to the events with all the passionate fervor of a true patriot, artist and citizen.

Between the end of June, 1941, and August, 1943, he composed three symphonies, three string quartets, a large work for solo voices, chorus and orchestra, an overture and two marches for brass band, two important pieces for the piano, and a number of songs. All this was in addition to his pedagogical and editorial work, to which he devoted, then as now, no little time and energy. At the same time, it should be remembered that eighteen months of these two years

123

were spent far from home for, in view of the frequent German raids on Moscow, the Soviet Government evacuated the leading members of the art and scientific world into the interior of the country. In the middle of July, 1941, Myaskovsky, with a group of other composers to which were attached the veteran actors of the Moscow Art and Maly Theatres, left Moscow for Kabardino-Balkaria in the North Caucasus, where he settled down for a time in the neighborhood of Nalchik.

Later he moved to Tbilisi, the capital of Georgia, and at the end of 1942 to Frunze (Kirghizia). In January, 1943, he returned to Moscow.

Although torn from his accustomed surroundings and obliged to give up a routine he had followed for many years, Myaskovsky retained his habit of systematic work. With a persistence and energy that were amazing under the circumstances, he applied himself to his music, producing a whole series of compositions in quick succession.

In little more than a fortnight following Hitler's attack on the Soviet Union, Myaskovsky wrote several songs on patriotic themes: *Marching Song*, for male chorus without accompaniment, to words by the poet M. Isakovsky (June 29), and two songs in ballad form, stern and martial in spirit —*Young Fighter*, for voice and piano, words by M. Svetlov (June 30), and *Fighting Orders*, for solo, chorus and piano accompaniment, words by V. Vinnikov (July 8).

During the first half of July, Myaskovsky also wrote two military marches in F minor and F major, Opus 53.

Between October and December, 1941, Myaskovsky wrote his 22nd Symphony ("Symphony-Ballad"), treating of the Patriotic War, his Seventh Quartet, and his 23rd Symphony, in the form of a suite on Kabardino-Balkarian themes.

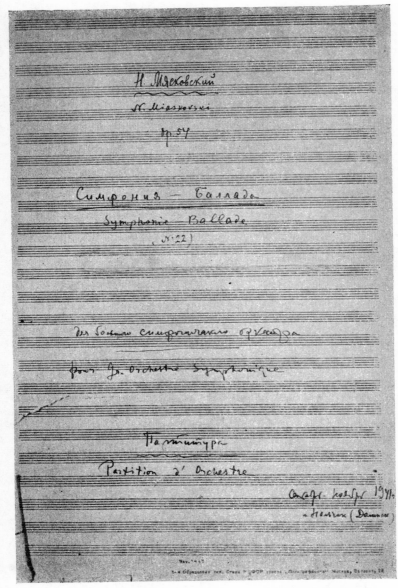

Figure 26. Autographed title page for the Symphony-Ballad (Symphony No. 22).

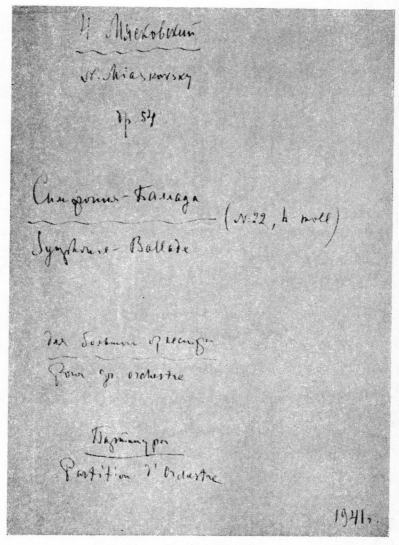

Figure 27. Autographed inner title page for the Symphony-Ballad
(Symphony No. 22).

While in Tbilisi he wrote a sonatina in E minor, a rhapsody in B-flat minor for piano (March, 1942), the Eighth Quartet (April–May, 1942) and an overture for brass band (June–July, 1942). In Frunze he wrote the draft of *Kirov Is With Us*, a cantata for solo voices, chorus and orchestra after the poem of the same title by Nikolai Tikhonov.

On his arrival at Moscow early in January, Myaskovsky put the finishing touches to the score of the "Kirov" cantata and worked on the transcription of several of his earlier works, including an arrangement for the pianoforte (four hands) of his 17th Symphony. Between April and September he composed his String Quartet No. 9, dedicated to the Beethoven Quartet, one of the oldest Soviet string ensembles, on the occasion of the twentieth anniversary of its foundation, and a large three-movement symphony in F minor, his 24th.

Such are the bare outlines of Myaskovsky's creative activities during the period of the Patriotic War. To them I propose to add a few words concerning the ideological and esthetic aspects of his work.

*   *   *

The 22nd Symphony, Opus 54, in B minor ("Symphony-Ballad"), is one of the first [1] major works of Soviet music which responded directly to the war against fascist Germany. (*Cf.* Figures 26 and 27.) Written in the first four or five months of the war, the symphony has no explicit subject or "program." It does not depict battle scenes even to the extent that this is possible in music. It reveals the inner world of the artist's own reactions to the grim events that befell his country and his people.

---

[1] Shostakovich's Seventh Symphony was completed in January, 1942.

The "Symphony-Ballad" is profoundly lyrical in the true
sense of the word; it is distinguished above all by its depth
and sincerity of feeling and the beauty and nobility of its
ideas.

It consists of three long movements which, though intrinsically independent of each other, are played without the
intervening pause customary for works of this length. By this
means the composer stresses the inherent unity of the upsurge
of varied emotions expressed in the music. Therein, indeed,
lies one of the specific features of the "symphony-ballad" form
which the author has chosen for his work, for he uses it, in
addition, to emphasize the epic nature of the symphony,
which is now contemplative and reflective, now tense and
dynamic.

The selection of musical images and the logic of their
development testify to the philosophical nature of the work,
to the composer's striving to generalize his ideas and emotional experiences.

The grave austerity and intensity of thought of the introduction seem to speak directly of war itself and of the frightful
suffering it causes.

But in fact this is not a portrayal of war: it is the composer's
thoughts about war. (Cf. Figure 28.) These thoughts recur
throughout the whole symphony: in the introduction, after
the exposition of the main themes of the first movement,
in its conclusion, in the transition to the second movement
and, lastly, in the finale. And each time they reappear it is as
though the composer returns to the world of reality, remind-
ing himself of what concerns and affects him most, namely—
the war.

The introduction is followed by an allegro in sonata form
(exposition-development-recapitulation), the first theme of

Figure 28. The introduction for the Symphony-Ballad (Symphony No. 22) (autograph).

which flows smoothly, gently and at the same time insistently
toward its goal. It is echoed by two charming lyrical images
(the subordinate theme) each of which is a continuation of
the other, and which are united by a common feeling of
exaltation, human kinship and Love—with a capital letter.

Figure 29. Second movement of the Symphony-Ballad
(Symphony No. 22).

In this movement the composer brings us back to the
serene and beautiful world of peaceful creative life, full of
inner movement. "This is life as it was," he tells us, and such,
in essence, is the idea of the entire movement. Only the theme
of the introduction that serves as its framework infringes on

the spirit of this beautiful world, thereby bringing out in sharper relief the thought that this is life *"as it was."*

The second movement, written in three-part form, presents images of profound sadness and sorrow (the first and last episodes) and a depiction of the invasion (central episode).

From the musical standpoint, the first and last episodes of the second movement are the best in the symphony. In them Myaskovsky has attained, by means of a simple melodic and harmonic formula in the spirit of a Russian lullaby, a depth and poignancy of feeling such as arise only in moments of genuine inspiration. (*Cf.* Figure 29.) The music of the middle episode, which I have called the "depiction of the invasion," is actually not so much a reproduction of scenes of the invasion, as the expression of a psychological state of gradually increasing tension rising to a climax of tremendous force (*fugato*). At the culmination of this episode the original theme of the second movement reappears. This time the image is conceived as an expression of impulsive passion, in which the dominant emotion is not so much sorrow as tragic, wrathful grief.

The finale of the "Symphony-Ballad" is presented and developed in an active, positive spirit, and culminates in a triumphant paean to victory. Its dynamic forcefulness springs above all from its principal theme, which is in march tempo and is built up on a series of insistent fanfare phrases with an impelling, regular rhythm. Although the main theme of the finale is preceded by similar fanfare-like passages, which prepare the way for it and create an atmosphere of impending battle, its ultimate advent is so powerful and striking that it seems to rend asunder the musical fabric of the whole. (*Cf.* Figure 30.) This impression is preserved throughout the finale with each recurrence of the main theme.

Figure 30. Third movement (finale) of the Symphony Ballad
(Symphony No. 22).

After its first masterful statement the paean to victory is broken off by a brief reminder of the introduction. But this echo of the opening image of war and calamity merely emphasizes the inevitable final triumph of the main theme as a symbol of the coming victory of mankind's lofty ideals over the forces of darkness and evil.

The "Symphony-Ballad" was first played in Tbilisi at the end of 1941 by the Tbilisi Philharmonic Orchestra conducted by Stasevich. In Moscow it was performed in the spring of 1942 by the orchestra of the All-Union Radio Committee under Professor Golovanov.

*   *   *

The 23rd Symphony ("Symphony-Suite"), Opus 56 (A minor–A major), is conceived on somewhat different lines.

This symphony was written under the direct influence of the composer's North Caucasian environment. It is based exclusively on Kabardino-Balkarian folk *motifs*. No other symphony by a Russian composer, with the exception of Glinka's, of which only the first movement is extant, has ever been written exclusively on folk themes. This alone would suffice to make the 23rd Symphony a significant and unusual work. It should be mentioned, moreover, that Myaskovsky has taken the greatest care to preserve all the innate peculiarities of the Kabardino-Balkarian songs and dances he used in an effort to reproduce the musical images in all their national integrity. At the same time, however, the symphony is by no means a simple ethnographical study in music, a mere anthology of folk tunes. It is, from the first note to the last, the fruit of Myaskovsky's creative genius.

In this symphony, indeed, the composer's personality may be said to merge with the specific features of the national

music. Hence its spirit of healthy optimism which has such
an appeal for us—particularly today, when the whole of our
people are united heart and soul in their mighty effort to
sweep the invader out of their native land.

The symphony consists of three movements, the first of
which is preceded by a brief introduction based on the broad
and tragic melody of an ancient Nart [2] song. This same
air recurs at the end of the movement and brings it to a
close.

The music of the introduction is contrasted to the leading
images of the first movement: the swift, lively tune of the
modern, heroic song *Vaksanstroi,* and the dynamic dance tune
Chetichezhev Ogurbi. Instead of elaborating these themes in
the middle episode of the first movement, however, Myaskovsky introduces a new musical image modeled on the
charming Kabardinian air *Saltan-Khamid,* which is remarkable both for its stern simplicity of melody and its soft, gentle
coloring.

In the second movement, which is at once lyrical and epic
in style, the composer develops three musical images, based
on two ancient Balkarian laments and a Kabardinian love
song.

The keynote of the finale is struck by the sparkling *Islamei*
folk dance. But besides the *Islamei,* the composer has drawn
upon the old Balkarian comic song *Khalimyat* and the Balkarian festive song *Arau Batai ak Batai* for his material in this
movement. The latter is perhaps worthy of especial attention
as a vivid example of the folk genre. In the melodious recitative speaks the voice of the minstrel rejoicing with the people.
The festive song episode, moreover, plays an important rôle

[2] A Caucasian nationality.

from the structural standpoint. Occupying as it does the central part of the finale, it calls a temporary halt in the dance theme and serves to prepare for its next wave, which is even more dynamic than the first and which crowns the whole movement.

The symphony was composed within the very brief period of ten days, a record even for Myaskovsky, who is known for the swift tempo at which he works. It would, however, be a mistake to attribute this speed to any hastiness or carelessness on the part of the composer. On the contrary, it was made possible precisely by his exhaustive preliminary labors. Before going on to the work of actual composition, Myaskovsky made a detailed and painstaking study of all the records of folk music at his disposal, listened to native bards and made a detailed analysis of the typical features of Kabardino-Balkarian songs.

In this, Myaskovsky reveals with especial clarity his firm ties with the best traditions of Russian classical music. "The people create music; we musicians merely arrange it." In this aphorism Glinka expressed one of the guiding principles of classic Russian national music.

This is the principle that is being observed in the best specimens of Soviet music today, to which category Myaskovsky's "Symphony-Suite" undoubtedly belongs.

The 23rd Symphony was first performed in Moscow in a radio broadcast on June 5, 1942, by the Grand Symphony Orchestra of the All-Union Radio Committee under the direction of Artist of Merit Professor Nikolai Golovanov.

*   *   *

Among the chamber works of the latter period mention should be made of the Seventh and Eighth String Quartets,

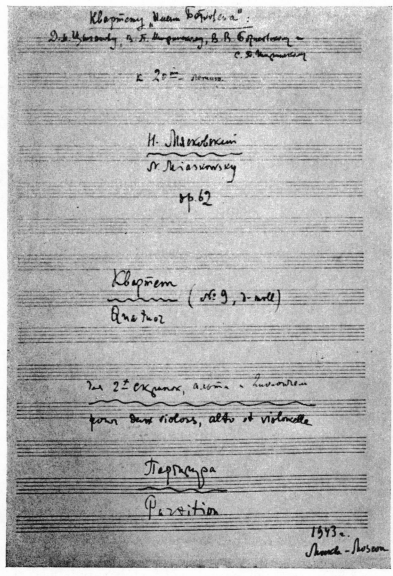

Figure 31. Title page for the score of the Quartet No. 9 (autograph).

Figure 32. First movement of the Quartet No. 9 (autograph).

which have won a prominent place in the repertories of Soviet chamber ensembles.

The Seventh Quartet in F major (October–November, 1941) is written in the style of the larger quartets of Glazounov and Taneyev. It is bright and almost entirely major in tone. Particularly successful in this respect is the first movement, which impresses the hearer by the unity of its lyricism and its gentle, caressing charm. It seems to have been written in one breath, so smoothy and evenly does the music develop. As a tribute to his sojourn in the North Caucasus Myaskovsky included one lyrical Kabardino-Balkarian folk song in the andante which adds a most refreshing touch to the movement. The last and fourth movement, which is the longest of all, is carried in rapid tempo to an effective and energetic conclusion. The Seventh Quartet is a highly individual work, full of charm and color, radiant in mood and readily accessible.

The Eighth Quartet in F-sharp minor (1942) is profoundly lyrical and tinged with a dash of sadness. A pervading wistfulness is the dominant mood of the first movement. In this movement Myaskovsky is reminiscent of Tchaikovsky, the Tchaikovsky of such romances as *Night* ("Oh, why do I love thee, radiant night?"), and the marked similarity of tone in this part of the quartet to the musical idiom of Tchaikovsky can scarcely have been a matter of chance. The andante, the second and perhaps the best movement of the Eighth Quartet, is solemn and contemplative in mood. Such moments in Myaskovsky's music are particularly impressive by virtue of the nobility and beauty of their musical ideas. A swift finale with an enchanting second theme rounds off the work.

I shall not attempt to dwell here in detail on Myaskovsky's

Figure 33. Second movement of the Quartet No. 9 (autograph).

Figure 34. Third movement (finale) of the Quartet No. 9
(autograph).

smaller-scale compositions of this period—his overture, military marches, sonatina and songs—since these works represent no departure either in content or form from the larger works.

*   *   *

Myaskovsky's cantata *Kirov Is With Us* for solo voices, chorus and orchestra was the last major work he produced outside of Moscow. It was conceived while the composer was still in Tbilisi and the rough draft was completed during his stay in Frunze, the capital of Kirghizia.

After the 23rd Symphony, the Seventh and Eighth Quartets, and a few pieces for the piano, Myaskovsky once again felt the need to respond more directly to the vital problems of the moment. His country was exerting herculean efforts to repulse the onslaught of the enemy. Immortal pages of courage and glory had been inscribed in the history of his people by the heroic cities of Sevastopol, Odessa, Leningrad, and Stalingrad, and miracles were being performed by men and women working in the rear. Art could not hold aloof from these themes, and artists eagerly sought to give expression to them.

Myaskovsky found the subject he was looking for in Tikhonov's inspired poem dedicated to Kirov and heroic Leningrad. This was during the time of the blockade. The steel ring of German trenches and fortifications was tightening round the city. The enemy was arrogantly confident of victory. But the indestructible will of the Soviet people, their scorn of death and their devotion to life and to the future of humanity, rose like an insurmountable barrier in the path of the armored fascist hordes. Beleaguered Leningrad became the heroic legend of an age.

Nikolai Tikhonov is a native of Leningrad. He has written

many splendid pages about the life and the people of this great city, and *Kirov Is With Us* is one of the most stirring of his poems. In it he gives an imposing and intensely human portrait of Sergei Kirov, fighter, statesman and leader, while at the same time he conveys the grim spirit of the city in blockade. It was these qualities in the poem that attracted Myaskovsky's attention and inspired him to write his cantata.

The very choice of the cantata form for a work of this kind is symptomatic. Only once before in his long career had Myaskovsky departed from the instrumental form: his Sixth Symphony, written in 1922–1923, twenty years before, has a chorus in the finale.

This advent of the cantata in Myaskovsky's work cannot be regarded as purely accidental, however much it may differ as a genre from the symphonic, his favorite form (this is also true for Myaskovsky's own Sixth Symphony, where the chorus is but an inserted episode: it sings a folk song and this ends its rôle in the symphony: in the cantata, however, the chorus is the very backbone of the work). The cantata is evidence of the profound evolution that has taken place in the composer's style, prominent landmarks in the development of which were such works as the 18th Symphony, called by the composer "songs without words," the 23rd Symphony on Kabardino-Balkarian themes, the 16th and 21st Symphonies and other works that are permeated with the song element.

It is thus in Myaskovsky's choice of theme and in the logical development of his style that the reasons for the advent of this—for him—new genre lie.

The "Kirov" cantata is a monumental heroic and patriotic work. Its music impresses the hearer by the integrity of its spirit of stern fortitude. At the same time, however, the epic and narrative passages alternate with moments of romantic fervor that run through the whole piece. Perhaps the most attractive feature of the cantata is its sense of proportion; nowhere is the epic quality over-accentuated or the exaltation exaggerated. Yet the emotional tension is preserved throughout.

A brief orchestral introduction presents the dominant themes of the cantata, which are subsequently woven into the fabric of the whole. The introduction begins with the theme of Kirov himself—an austere and noble melody in slow march time which is first rendered by the strings and woodwinds playing in unison in the low registers. Then we hear slow, *legato* chords played by the French horns within the framework of the main key (this same device strikes a somber, sinister note in the first movement and is used to create a feeling of tense expectation in the second movement). These are followed by an expressive descending melody, alternately passing from flutes to oboes and clarinets, against a sustained harmonic background of the strings. The latter impresses itself on the mind of the listener by virtue of the regularly alternating intervals (semitone—whole tone) of the descending scale. Its purpose is to suggest the emptiness and desolation of the settings of the first movement *City at Night*. One might point to the similarity between this passage, particularly with regard to the melody, and the orchestral prelude to Russlan's aria "Oh, thou field" in Glinka's *Russlan and Ludmilla*. Lastly, in the music of the introduction to the cantata one can already detect the characteristic rhythms of the entire work, now that measured march beat used by the composer to develop the image of Kirov leading the people of Leningrad forever onwards, now the flowing, smooth rhythm of the narrative in triple time.

There are four movements in the cantata: *City .at Night,
Factory, Kirov* and the finale *Battle*.

The orchestral prelude and the introductory phrase of the
chorus in the first movement:

> The darkened façades of buildings
> Stand hushed in ominous sleep . . .

depict the tense silence of the beleaguered city interrupted
by the flashes of nocturnal fighting:

> The sirens call to action
> And bombs whistle over the Neva,
> Searing the bridges with fire.

The introductory chorus is followed, after a brief orchestral
interlude on the Kirov theme, by a description of Kirov rendered by the chorus in a style akin to that of Schumann's
ballads (e.g., *The Two Grenadiers*) or Glinka's *Night
Review*:

> In the midst of the nightly alarm
> In the steel and lead of Leningrad nights
> Walks Kirov. . . .

This is one of the most enchantingly warm and moving
episodes in the cantata.

The figure of Kirov, who is introduced by the chorus in
the manner of a Greek tragedy, runs through the whole
cantata. The first movement begins and ends with the Kirov
theme, and it recurs at the beginning of both the third movement and (in a slightly modified form) of the finale.

The central episode of the first movement, framed by the
chorus which treats of Kirov himself, tells the story of a

young Baltic sailor from the *Kirov* battleship who personifies the hero.

Its calm, flowing melody (mezzo-soprano solo) in radiant major tone depicts the nobility, youth and strength of the sailor who stands on guard over his beloved Leningrad.

A similar arrangement occurs in the second movement. After painting the background of the factory, with its underlying incessant hum of machinery, and conveying the spirit of tense concentration on the part of the workers who are tirelessly forging the weapons of victory (chorus), the composer passes on to a monologue by an old worker (solo baritone) expounding the credo of the people of Leningrad: the enemy shall not pass!

> This shall never be.
> On the sacred banks of the Neva
> We, the working folk of Russia,
> Shall die rather than surrender.

There is a strong dramatic element in the factory scene and particularly in the monologue of the old worker. But the composer carefully avoids any exaggeration. Correctly grasping the essence of the heroism of the Soviet people, the simplicity and directness of their emotions and behavior, he has succeeded in infusing into his music the proper proportions of warmth, lyricism, and exaltation.

The third movement is dedicated directly to Kirov, the statesman and warrior, the man with an adamant yet tender heart, who went through many bitter trials and who loved

> With his last great love
> Great toiling Leningrad.

This movement takes the form of a duet (mezzo-soprano and baritone) with chorus. It opens with the chorus repeating the Kirov theme as in the first movement:

> In the steel and lead of Leningrad nights
> Walks Kirov. . . .

The chorus gives color and variety to the cantata. In Myaskovsky's hands the chorus with its mighty volume of sound becomes an effective means of giving emotional depth to the portrait of Kirov. The chorus, above all, is used in a masterly way to build up the climax of the finale.

From the very opening of the finale Myaskovsky strikes a note of agitation and alarm. As the text develops he brings the music to the highest pitch of emotional tensity, culminating with the resounding paean to victory:

> Tanks from the snowy ploughlands
> Rumble heavily off to war.
> "For country!" reads the legend on a turret;
> "Kirov" is inscribed on another.
> The scarlet banner,
> Like the banner of victory, flutters above them
> And Kirov's name
> Leads the men of Leningrad on!

The triumphant conclusion in major tone by full chorus and orchestra is like a dazzling shaft of sunlight breaking through the storm clouds.

The logical devolopment of the music, its intrinsically symphonic nature, the simplicity and emotional sincerity of its images, the masterful use of the solo voices and chorus coupled with colorful and effective orchestration—all these qualities combine to create a stirring and powerful piece of music.

Kirov Is With Us is Russian national music of the Great Patriotic War. It cannot fail to move anyone who is not entirely impervious to true beauty.

This cantata will take its place in Soviet music as a document of the heroic art of the Great Patriotic War. It was first performed over the air on November 27, 1943, by the All-Union Radio Committee orchestra conducted by A. Kovalev, with A. Kuvykin leading the chorus. The soloists were Tamara Yanko, of the Stanislavsky and Nemirovich-Danchenko Opera Theatre, and Vladimir Zakharov, of the All-Union Radio Committee.

*   *   *

This review of Myaskovsky's work does not pretend to completeness. Nor can it, for the composer has not passed the zenith of his creative powers, and his work is only beginning to be fully appreciated by the world at large. Only the future can pass final judgment on it.

Catalogue of Myoskovsky's Works

MYASKOVSKY'S WORKS

I. ORCHESTRAL WORKS

A. For Full Orchestra

1908, 1921.   Op. 3.   Symphony No. 1 in C minor, three movements, for symphony orchestra. Music Dept. of State Publishing House, 1929.

1909.   (No opus number.)   *Petite Ouverture* in G major. MS.

1909.   Op. 9.   *The Vow of Silence,* allegorical tone poem in F minor, subject from Edgar Allan Poe, for enlarged symphony orchestra with quadrupled strings and harps. Univ. Edit., 1925.

1910–1911.   Op. 11.   Symphony No. 2 in C-sharp minor, three movements, for enlarged symphony orchestra, with tripled strings, 4 trumpets, 2 tubas and 6 horns. Music Dept. of State Publishing House, 1928.

1912.   Op. 14.   *Alastor,* tone poem in C minor, subject from Shelley, for symphony orchestra, with tripled strings, 6 horns, celesta, and 2 harps. Music Dept. of State Publishing House, 1922.

1913.   Op. 15.   Symphony No. 3 in A minor, two movements, for symphony orchestra, with tripled strings and 6 horns. Music Dept. of State Publishing House, 1927.

1917–1918.   Op. 17.   Symphony No. 4 in E minor, three movements, for symphony orchestra, with tripled strings and 6 horns. Music Dept. of State Publishing House, 1926.

1918–1919.   Op. 18.   Symphony No. 5 in D major, four movements, for symphony orchestra, with tripled strings and 6 horns. Music Dept. of State Publishing House, 1923.

1922–1923.   Op. 23.   Symphony No. 6 in E-flat minor, four movements, for symphony orchestra, with tripled strings, 6 horns, celesta, and harp, and mixed chorus. Univ. Edit., 1925.

1922. Op. 24. Symphony No. 7 in B minor, two movements, for symphony orchestra, with tripled strings, 4 horns, 2 trumpets and harp. Univ. Edit., 1926.

1923–1925. Op. 26. Symphony No. 8 in A major, four movements, for symphony orchestra, with tripled strings, 6 horns and harp. Univ. Edit., 1927.

1926. Op. 28. Symphony No. 9 in E minor, four movements, for symphony orchestra, with tripled strings, 4 horns and harp, without double bassoon. Univ. Edit., 1928.

1927. Op. 30. Symphony No. 10 in F minor, one movement, for symphony orchestra, with quadrupled strings. Music Dept. of State Publishing House, 1929.

1931. Op. 34. Symphony No. 11 in B-flat minor, three movements, for symphony orchestra, with tripled strings and 4 horns, without double bassoon. State Music Publishing House, 1934.

1931. Op. 35. Symphony No. 12 in G minor, three movements, for symphony orchestra, with tripled strings and 4 horns, without double bassoon. State Music Publishing House, 1932.

1933. Op. 36. Symphony No. 13 in B-flat minor, one movement, for symphony orchestra, with tripled strings and 4 horns, without double bassoon. MS.

1933. Op. 37. Symphony No. 14 in C major, five movements, for symphony orchestra, with tripled strings and 4 horns, without double bassoon. State Music Publishing House, 1937.

1933–1934. Op. 38. Symphony No. 15 in D minor, four movements, for symphony orchestra, with tripled strings and 4 horns, without double bassoon. State Music Publishing House, 1937.

1907, 1934. (No opus number.) *Preludio e fughetta* in G minor on the name "Saradgef," for symphony orchestra with 3 trumpets. MS.

1935–1936. Op. 39. Symphony No. 16 in F minor, four movements, for symphony orchestra with tripled strings, without double bassoon. State Music Publishing House, 1939.

1936–1937. Op. 41. Symphony No. 17 in G-sharp minor, four movements, for symphony orchestra, with tripled strings, double bassoon, harp, xylophone, etc. MS.

1937. Op. 42. Symphony No. 18 in C major, three movements, for symphony orchestra, with 3 trumpets. State Music Publishing House, 1939.

1939. Op. 48. *Greetings Overture* in C major, for symphony orchestra. MS.

1940. Op. 50. Symphony No. 20 in E major, three movements, for grand orchestra, with tripled strings. MS.

1940. Op. 51. Symphony No. 21 in F-sharp minor, one movement, for grand orchestra, with tripled strings. State Cinematographic Publishing House and Union of Soviet Composers, 1940.

1941. Op. 54. Symphony No. 22 in B minor ("Symphony-Ballad"), three movements without break, for grand symphony orchestra. MS.

1941. Op. 56. Symphony No. 23 in A minor ("Symphony-Suite") on Kabardino-Balkarian themes, three movements, for grand symphony orchestra. MS.

1942. Op. 61. Cantata *Kirov Is With Us* in D minor, four movements, for grand symphony orchestra, with mezzo-soprano, baritone and mixed chorus. MS. (Pfte. score in publication.)

1943. Op. 63. Symphony No. 24 in F minor, three movements, for grand symphony orchestra. MS.

B. For Small Orchestra, or Specific Combinations

1910. Op. 10. *Sinfonietta* in A major, for small symphony orchestra, without trombones. MS.

1928. Op. 32, No. 1. *Serenade* in E-flat major, three movements, for small orchestra, without trombones. State Music Publishing House, 1930.

1928–1929. Op. 32, No. 2. *Sinfonietta* in B minor, three movements, for string orchestra. State Music Publishing House, 1931.

1929. Op. 32, No. 3. *Lyrical Concertino* in G major, three movements, for woodwinds, harp and strings. State Music Publishing House, 1930.

C. For Brass Band

1930. Two military marches:
  1. *The Solemn,* B-flat major. State Music Publishing House, 1930.
  2. *The Dramatic,* F major. State Music Publishing House, 1931.

1939. Op. 46. Symphony No. 19 in E-flat major, four movements.
MS.

1941. Op. 53. Two marches:
No. 1 in F minor. In publication.
No. 2 in F major. In publication.

1942. Op. 60. Overture in G minor. In publication.

II. CHAMBER MUSIC

A. String Quartets

1907. (No opus number). F major, four movements. MS.

1909–1910. Op. 33, No. 4. F minor, four movements. Revised
1936. State Music Publishing House, 1937.

1910. Op. 33, No. 3. D minor, two movements. State Music Publishing House, 1931.

1929–1930. Op. 33, No. 1. A minor, four movements. State Music
Publishing House, 1932.

1930. Op. 33, No. 2. C minor, three movements. State Music Publishing House, 1931.

1939. Op. 47. Quartet No. 5 in E minor, four movements. State
Music Publishing House, 1940.

1939–1940. Op. 49. Quartet No. 6 in G minor, four movements.
State Publishing House, 1941.

1941. Op. 55. Quartet No. 7 in F major, four movements. In publication.

1942. Op. 59. Quartet No. 8 in F-sharp minor, three momevents.
In publication.

1943. Op. 62. Quartet No. 9 in E minor, three movements. In publication.

B. Miscellaneous

1911. Op. 12. Sonata in D major for Violoncello and Pianoforte.
Jurgenson, 1913; State Music Publishing House, 1924; revised
1931, in publication.

1938. Op. 44. Concerto in D minor for Violin, three movements.
State Music Publishing House, 1939 (pfte. score).

III. PIANOFORTE WORKS

1907–1909. Op. 6. Sonata No. 1 in D minor, in four movements. Jurgenson, 1919; Music Dept. of State Publishing House, 1924.

1912. Op. 13. Sonata No. 2 in F-sharp minor, one movement. Jurgenson, 1913; Music Dept. of State Publishing House, 1924.

1920. Op. 19. Sonata No. 3 in C minor, one movement. Music Dept. of State Publishing House, 1923. Revised 1939.

1922. Op. 25. *Whimsies,* six sketches for the pianoforte. Russian Music Publishing House, 1923.
1. A minor (1917).
2. B minor (1917).
3. B-flat minor (1917).
4. A minor (1917).
5. G minor (1917).
6. F-sharp major (1919).

1924. Op. 27. Sonata No. 4 in C minor, three movements (second movement—1917). Univ. Edit., 1925.

1927. Op. 29. *Reminiscences,* six pieces for the pianoforte. Univ. Edit., 1928; State Music Publishing House.
1. *Air* (1907).
2. *Jest* (1907).
3. *Despair* (1907).
4. *Recollection* (1907).
5. *Sleepless* (1907).
6. *Snow Wraith* (1907).

1928. Op. 31. *Yellowed Leaves,* seven *bagatelles* for the pianoforte. Music Dept. of State Publishing House, 1930.
1. E minor (1917).
2. C minor (1907).
3. E minor (1907).
4. C major (1906).
5. A-flat major (1917).
6. D minor (1917).
7. B-flat minor (1906).

1938. Op. 43. Three Albums of Children's Pieces. State Music Publishing House, 1938.
1. Ten very easy pieces (1908, 1917, 1938).
2. Four little polyphonic pieces (1907).
3. Simple variations (1908).

1942.   Op. 57.   Sonatina in E minor, in three movements. State
Music Publishing House, 1943.
1942.   Op. 58.   Rhapsody for the pianoforte in B-flat minor. State
Music Publishing House, 1943.

Without Opus Number

1899–1901.   Seven preludes, MS.
    1.   G major (1899).
    2.   D major (1899).
    3.   A-flat major (1899).
    4.   E minor (1899).
    5.   F-sharp minor (1900).
    6.   D major (1900).
    7.   C-sharp minor (1901).
1906.   *Espiègleries* (*Frolics*), Part I, six sketches for the pianoforte.
MS.
    1.   *Prélude.*
    2.   *Menuet.*
    3.   *Chant* (*Cf.* third movement of Ninth Symphony, Op. 28).
    4.   *Scherzo* (*Yellowed Leaves, Op. 31, No. 4*).
    5.   *Légende.*
    6.   *Bagatelle.*
1906–1907.   *Espiègleries* (*Frolics*), Part II, six sketches for the pianoforte. MS.
    1.   *Fête profane* (1906).
    2.   *Chant apocryphe* (1906. *Yellowed Leaves, Op. 31, No. 7*).
    3.   *Gavotte* (1907).
    4.   *Plein air* (1907. *Cf.* second movement of *Sinfonietta* in
A major, Op. 10).
    5.   *Rigaudon* (1907).
    6.   *Fuguette* (1907. *Cf. Preludio e fughetta*).
1907.   *Espiègleries* (*Frolics*), Part III, twelve sketches for the pianoforte. MS.
    1.   *Préludiette* (*Reminiscences, Op. 29, No. 1*).
    2.   *Danse burlesque.*
    3.   *Valsette* (*Reminiscences, Op. 29, No. 4*).
    4.   *Berceuse* (*Reminiscences, Op. 29, No. 5*).
    5.   *Bouderie.*

6. *Aux champs.*
7. *Pensée.*
8. *Désespoir* (*Reminiscences*, Op. 29, No. 3).
9. *Marche.*
10. *L'oiseau.*
11. *Barcarolle.*
12. *Scherzo* (*Reminiscences*, Op. 29, No. 2).

1907–1908. Twenty-five fugues (student work). Eleven of these are on themes by Myaskovsky himself. Three are included in the Second Album of Children's Pieces, Op. 43, No. 2. MS.

1907–1908. Pianoforte Sonata in B major, five movements; first, second, third and fifth movements—1907, fourth movement—1908. MS. Last edited 1917.

1907–1908. *Espiègleries* (*Frolics*), Part IV, twelve sketches for the pianoforte. State Music Publishing House, 1938.

1. *Duettino* (1907. Three Albums of Children's Pieces, Op. 43, No. 2).
2. *Mélancolie* (1907. *Yellowed Leaves*, Op. 31, No. 2).
3. *Chant* (1907. *Yellowed Leaves*, Op. 31, No. 3).
4. *Grotesque* (1907).
5. *Nocturne* (1907).
6. *Rêves d'hiver* (1907. *Reminiscences*, Op. 29, No. 6).
7. *Phrase* (1907).
8. *Madrigal* (1907).
9. *Interlude* (1907).
10. *Idylle* (1907).
11. *Conte mystique* (1908. Three Albums of Children's Pieces, Op. 43, No. 1).
12. *Variations intimes* (1908).

1908. Pianoforte Sonata in A-flat major, one movement. MS. Last edited 1925.

1908. *Espiègleries* (*Frolics*), Part V, three sketches for the pianoforte. MS.

1. *Toccatina.*
2. *Reproche.*
3. *Cortège.*

1909–1912. *Espiègleries* (*Frolics*), Part VI, three sketches for the pianoforte. MS.

1. *Mazurka* (1909).
2. *Esquisse* (1910).

3. *Epilogue* (1912. Cf. third movement of 15th Symphony, Op. 38).

1917–1919.   *Frolics*, Part VII, nineteen sketches for the pianoforte. MS.

    1. *To Sleep* (1917).
    2. *Whimsies* (1917).
    3. *Close of a Song* (1917).
    4. *Controversy* (1917. *Yellowed Leaves,* Op. 31, No. 6).
    5. *Despair* (1917).
    6. *Strange Procession* (1917. *Whimsies,* Op. 25, No. 2).
    7. *Echoes* (1917).
    8. *Dejection* (1917).
    9. *Conflict* (1917).
    10. *Intuitions* (1917. *Whimsies,* Op. 25, No. 4).
    11. *Tocsin* (1917).
    12. *Reflection* (1917).
    13. *Dissatisfaction* (1917. *Whimsies,* Op. 25, No. 3).
    14. *Fairy Tale* (1917. *Whimsies,* Op. 25, No. 1).
    15. *Jest* (1917. *Whimsies,* Op. 25, No. 5).
    16. *Call* (1917).
    17. *Apathy* (1917. *Yellowed Leaves,* Op. 31, No. 1).
    18. *A la sarabande* (1917. Pianoforte Sonata No. 4 in C minor, second movement, Op. 27).
    19. *Left Unsaid* (1919. *Whimsies,* Op. 25, No. 6).

IV.   VOCAL WORKS

A.   Choral

1909.   *Feather-Grass,* for four-part mixed chorus, unaccompanied, words by Balmont. MS.

1931.   *Wings of the Soviets,* for two-part mass chorus, with pianoforte accompaniment, words by N. Aseyev. State Music Publishing House, 1932.

1931.   *In Valor's Name,* for two-part mass chorus, words by I. Frenkel. State Music Publishing House, 1932.

1931.   *Planes Are Flying,* for two-part mass chorus, words by I. Stroganov. State Music Publishing House, 1932.

1932–1933.   *Lenin* ("In the grey expanses . . ."), for mass chorus in unison, with pianoforte accompaniment, words by A. Surkov. State Music Publishing House, 1933.

1932. *Karl Marx*, for two-part chorus, with pianoforte accompaniment, words by S. Kirsanov. State Music Publishing House, 1933.

1934. *Partisans* ("The sap stirred in the poplars . . ."), for mass chorus in unison, with pianoforte accompaniment, words by S. Ostrovoy. State Music Publishing House, 1934.

1934. *Marching Song* ("The columns pass over the fields . . ."), for mass chorus in unison, with pianoforte accompaniment, words by A. Surkov. State Music Publishing House, 1935.

1934. *Song of the Border-Guards*, for two-part mass chorus, with pianoforte accompaniment, words by V. Vinnikov. State Music Publishing House, 1935.

1934. *Glory to Our Soviet Pilots*, for four part mixed chorus, unaccompanied, words by A. Surkov. State Music Publishing House, 1934.

1941. *Marching Song*, for men's chorus, unaccompanied, words by M. Isakovsky. MS.

1941. *Fighting Orders*, for voice and chorus, with pianoforte, accompaniment, words by V. Vinnikov. MS.

B. For Voice With Accompaniment

1907. Op. 1. *Meditations*, seven * pieces to words by Baratynsky, for voice and pianoforte. Music Dept. of State Publishing House, 1922.
   1. "Modest my gift . . ."
   2. *Marvellous City*.
   3. *Muse*.
   4. *Ailing Soul*.
   5. "Once upon a time, a lad . . ."
   6. *Naiad*.
   7. "The enchantment of the beauty in thee . . ."

1904–1906. Op. 2. *On the Threshold*, nine pieces to words by Zinaida Gippius, for voice and pianoforte. Music Dept. of State Publishing House, 1922. (Published as Op. 22, but later rejected by the composer.)
   1. *Leeches* (1904).
   2. *Nothing* (1904).
   3. *Spiders* (1904).

---

* No. 4 was later excluded by the composer.

4. *Inscription in a Book* (1905).
5. *Instant* (1905).
6. *Lands of Despondency* (1905).
7. *Inscription on an Envelope* (1905).
8. *Dust* (1906).
9. *Flower of the Night* (1906).

1905–1908. Op. 4. Three songs for voice and pianoforte to words by Zinaida Gippius. Russian Music Publishing House, 1913. Published without opus number.

    1. *Contradiction* (1905).
    2. *Monotony* (1906).
    3. *Circles* (1908).

1904–1908. Op. 5. *Unseen,* four pieces to words by Zinaida Gippius, for voice and pianoforte. Published without opus number, but later rejected by the composer.

    1. *The Moon and the Mist* (1905). Jurgenson, 1912; State Music Publishing House, 1921.
    2. *Blood* (1908). Jurgenson, 1912; State Music Publishing House, 1921.
    3. *In the Parlor* (1904). Revised 1913. Jurgenson, 1915; State Music Publishing House, 1921.
    4. "To no sad teacher . . ." (1906). Jurgenson, 1915; State Music Publishing House, 1921.

1908–1909. Op. 7. *Madrigal,* suite to words by Balmont, for voice and pianoforte. (Subsequently published by Univ. Edit.)

    1. Prelude, "Oh, in the spirit . . ." (1908).
    2. Romance, "Thou art the rustle of the tender leaf . . ." (1908).
    3. Interlude, "Oh, in the spirit . . ." (1909).
    4. Romance, "Thine azure eyes . . ." (1908).
    5. Postlude, "Oh, in the spirit . . ." (1909).

1908. Op. 8a. Three sketches for voice and pianoforte, to words by Ivanov. Russian Music Publishing House, 1913. Published without opus number.

    1. *The Storm.*
    2. *Temple-Valley.*
    3. *Pan and Psyche.*

1909. Op. 8b. *Sonnet,* for voice and pianoforte, to words by Michelangelo (transl. Tyutchev). Russian Music Publishing House, 1910.

1913–1914. Op. 16. *Premonitions,* six pieces for voice and piano-

forte to words by Zinaida Gippius. Jurgenson, 1915; State Music
Publishing House, 1921; Univ. Edit., 1928; later rejected by composer.

1. *Gift* (1913).
2. *Pain* (1913).
3. *Is It So?* (1913).
4. *Incantation* (1913).
5. *Unawares* (1913).
6. *The Cocks* (1914).

1921. Op. 20. Six pieces for voice and pianoforte to words by
Blok. Music Dept. of State Publishing House, 1922.

1. *A Full Moon.*
2. *Dear Friend.*
3. *In Slow Succession.*
4. "I rise in the misty morning . . ." *
5. "Frightful is the cold of eve . . ."
6. "In the stilly night . . ."

1922. Op. 21. *At the Close of Day,* three sketches for voice and
pianoforte to words by Tyutchev. Music Dept. of State Publishing House, 1923.

1. "It is not given us to foretell . . ." †
2. "Your voice no more awakes . . ."
3. "Let the last hour be ne'er so grim . . ."

1925. Op. 22. *Faded Garland,* eight pieces for voice and pianoforte
to words by Delvig. Music Dept. of State Publishing House, 1926.

1. "Why write in thy tablets?"
2. "Why so dejected, shepherd lass?"
3. *Love.*
4. *Lovers' Nearness* (from Goethe).
5. *Skylark.*
6. "No, I am not yours . . ."
7. "What, does thy heart not grieve thee?"
8. *Tableau d'automne.*

1935–1936. Op. 40. Twelve pieces for voice and pianoforte to
words by Lermontov. State Music Publishing House, 1937.

1. *Cossack Lullaby* (1935).
2. "Alone I go forth into the road . . ." (1935).

---

* Later excluded by the composer.
† Later excluded by the composer.

3. "No, it is not you I love with such ardor . . ." (1936).
4. *To a Portrait* ("Frolicsome as a curly-headed boy . . .") (1936).
5. The Sun (1936).
6. "They loved each other . . ." (1936).
7. "Like a lonely sepulchre . . ." ("From an album") (1936).
8. *Romance* ("You are leaving for the wars . . .") (1936).
9. "She sings . . ." (1936).
10. "Weep not, my dear one . . ." (1936).
11. "I also loved in days gone by . . ." ("From an album") (1936).
12. "Farewell! We shall not meet again . . ." (1936).

1938. Op. 45. Three sketches for voice and pianoforte to words by Shchipachev and Kvitko. In publication.
1. *Flowerlet* (Shchipachev).
2. *The Birch Tree* (Shchipachev).
3. *Conversation* (Kvitko, transl. Mikhalkov).

1940. Op. 52. Ten pieces for voice and pianoforte to words by Shchipachev. State Music Publishing House, 1941.
1. *Russet Wind.*
2. *By the Spring.*
3. "Sometimes I think . . ."
4. *Sunflower.*
5. *Token.*
6. *To You.*
7. "Sweetly, my love, with thee . . ."
8. *Elbruss and the 'Plane.*
9. "Glancing at your photo . . ."
10. *By the Sea.*

Without Opus Number

1901. "The spirit so bursts forth . . .", words by A. Koltsov. MS.
1903. *Lullaby* ("The light wind falls . . ."), words by Balmont. MS. Revised 1925.
1903. *Bas-Relief,* words by A. Golenishchev-Kutuzov. MS.
1903. "I extinguished the fire . . .", words by L. Yarmonkina. MS.
1903. "Raising its head above the waters . . .", words by A. K. Tolstoy. MS.

1904. *Twilight,* words by Ferrari. MS.
1904. Six pieces for voice and pianoforte to words by Balmont. MS.
Edited 1925.
    1. "Somewhere the boom of waves died down . . ."
    2. "The night grew pale . . ."
    3. "The moon at midnight . . ."
    4. "From beyond distant seas . . ."
    5. *Night by the Sea.*
    6. *Flowerlet.*
1904–1905. Four pieces for voice and pianoforte to words by Zinaida
Gippius. MS. Edited 1925.
    1. *Serenade* (1904).
    2. *The Knock* (1905).
    3. *The Christian* (1905).
    4. *Another Christian* (1905).
1906. Five pieces for voice and pianoforte to words by Balmont.
MS. Edited 1925.
    1. *The Albatross.*
    2. "I am lost in dreams . . ."
    3. "Come, death, lull me to sleep . . ."
    4. *Sphinx.*
    5. "God will not remember them . . ."
1906. *Song of the Gatherers,* words by V. Bryusov. MS. Edited
1925.
1908. "At grips with bitter fate . . .", words by Baratynsky. MS.
1908. "Thoughts, always thoughts . . .", words by Baratynsky.
MS.
1908. *Limit,* words by Zinaida Gippius. MS.
1908. "As May's blue-eyed . . .", words by A. Fet. MS.
1908. "I do not grieve . . ." words by Edgar Allan Poe. MS.
1930. Two collective-farm songs for voice with pianoforte accompaniment. MS.
    1. *Song,* words by Nasedkin.
    2. *Collective-Farm Autumn,* words by Yerikeyev.
1934. Four songs of the Arctic explorers.
    1. *Song of Pride,* words—anon. MS.
    2. *Song,* words by M. Svetlov. MS.
    3. *Song,* words by M. Svetlov (second version). MS.
    4. *Song of the Arctic Sailor,* words by Zelvensky. State Music
Publishing House, 1940.

1936.   Spanish cradle song for voice and pianoforte ("Sleep, my child; sleep, little Pancho . . ."), words by T. Sikorskaya. MS.

1936.   *Song From the Bottom of My Heart* (on Stalin), for voice and pianoforte, words by the Kazakh national bard Jambul. State Music Publishing House, 1937.

1936.   *To Romain Rolland,* for voice and pianoforte, words by Kasim Lakuti. State Music Publishing House, 1939.

1941.   *Young Fighter,* for voice with pianoforte accompaniment, words by M. Svetlov. MS.